Beat the House

Beat the House

16

Ways to Win at Blackjack, Roulette, Craps, Baccarat and Other Casino Games

Frederick Lembeck

A Citadel Press Book
Published by Carol Publishing Group

To Morton Cole, My Pa

A Citadel Press Book
Published by Carol Publishing Group
Citadel Press is a registered trademark of Carol Communications, Inc.
Editorial Offices: 600 Madison Avenue, New York, N.Y. 10022
Sales and Distribution Offices: 120 Enterprise Avenue, Secaucus, N.J. 07094
In Canada: Canadian Manda Group, One Atlantic Avenue, Suite 105, Toronto, Ontario, M6K 3E7
Queries regarding rights and permissions should be addressed to Carol Publishing Group, 600 Madison Avenue, New York, N.Y. 10022

Carol Publishing Group books are available at special discounts for bulk purchases, sales promotion, fund-raising, or educational purposes. Special editions can be created to specification. For details, contact: Special Sales Department, Carol Publishing Group, 120 Enterprise Avenue, Secaucus, N.J. 07094

Manufactured in the United States of America
10 9 8 7 6 5 4 3 2 1

Library of Congress Cataloging-in-Publication Data

Lembeck, Frederick.
  Beat the house : sixteen ways to win at blackjack, roulette, baccarat, and other casino games / by Frederick Lembeck.
      p.   cm.
  "A Citadel Press book."
  ISBN 0-8065-1607-0 (pbk.)
  1. Gambling systems.   2. Gambling.   I. Title.
GV1302.L38   1995
795'.01—dc20   94-46169
                                           CIP

Contents

Part V: Hedging Craps

Part VI: Hedging Roulette

Part VII: Capital

Part VIII: Still More Systems

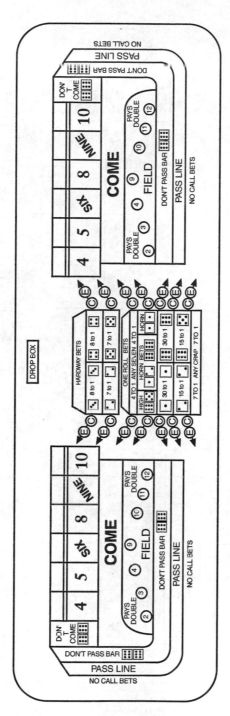

The Craps Layout

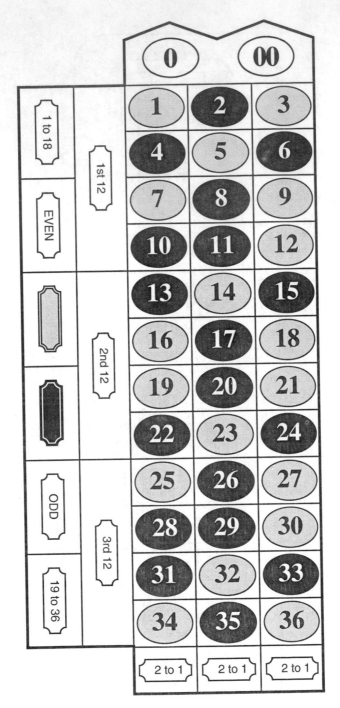

The Roulette Layout

I

Progressive Gambling Systems

1

Progressive Gambling Systems

The mathematical systems in this book are all just scaled down versions of the basic systems Wall Street institutional investors have been using for years to milk the stock market.

You begin by recognizing that a craps table or roulette wheel is only superficially a game of chance. On a deeper level it's a toy stock exchange. The only difference is that instead of price changes responding to something the president or the Federal Reserve board did, they respond to what the dice or the wheel did. Sometimes the prices are up, sometimes they're down, but they're always in motion and this is where a mathematical system's profit comes from, this endless up-down motion, the fact that it's not following random chance the way the true gamblers are, it's following a *progression*. This is a well-known phenomenon in the real-world stock markets. It's called *dollar cost averaging*. Instead of buying his stock in one lump and hoping the price goes up, the dollar cost averager buys and sells his shares in small dribbles, selling ever-increasing amounts any time the price is rising and buying ever-increasing amounts any time the price is falling. To him it's a matter of complete indifference whether the price of his stock is going up or down. If it's going up, he sells a few shares at a relative profit; if it's going down, he buys a few shares at a relative bargain. This kind of operator makes out no matter which way the market's going, and the same principle applies to the more elegant casino systems: you're going to lose some of the time, and you're going to win some of the time, but nobody loses all the time, any more than anybody wins all the time. The idea, both on the stock exchanges and in the casinos, is to follow a logical progression over time, buying more shares when you're losing so you'll have that many more shares to sell when you're winning.

This is what separates a mathematical system player from the gamblers who bet on random chance. For a system player, the bets on the craps table or roulette wheel aren't bets, they're investment positions. They're not one-shot encounters with random chance but thoughtful, carefully managed investment positions to be adjusted steadily over the course of time, with the amount of each new bet determined by whether he won or lost on the previous bet. The system player doesn't care if he's winning or losing anymore than the dollar cost averager cares if stock prices are going up or down. When he loses, it's a chance to increase the size of his bet so he'll win that much more when his luck changes. When he wins, it's a chance to decrease the size of his bet so he'll lose that much less when his luck changes. And all the while he's constantly winning slightly more than he's losing—because when he wins, he always wins more than the amount he just lost, and when he loses, he always loses less than the amount he just won.

After you've tried it out on the kitchen table with the dice from your Monopoly set, it'll all be much clearer to you. This is an essential part of learning how. You must *practice.* Do you remember how Van Cliburn practiced for the Tschaikovsky Competition before leaving for Moscow? That's how you have to practice before leaving for the casino. Use pennies to represent $1 chips, nickels $5 chips, dimes $10, etc. Be totally and thoroughly familiar with the systems long before you go forth to Atlantic City, Las Vegas, or wherever. The casino floor is no place for training. On the casino floor, with real money, it's more like being in a war zone with real bullets. You must have all your training behind you before you try to do it for real. There's no substitute for practice. You must know the systems *cold* before you ever set foot in the casino.

2

A Great Mystery

There's more to it than that, however. You're going to discover right away that the systems work very well at home and you're going to make lots of money with them at your kitchen table, but when you try to use them in the casinos, you're going to discover that they don't work nearly as well. Why is this so? I don't know. It's a great mystery. For some unknown reason the law of probability is much harsher in casinos than it is at your kitchen table.

Now I have to explain at this point that my wise and gentle editor, in our discussions prior to the final draft of this book, asked me not to suggest that casinos are using rigged tables or anything like that. He did allow I could present the systems, along with an accompanying story, and then let my readers decide what to make of it all. Therefore, you get a story as well as some gambling systems that work impressively well at home. But the story isn't so much a drama as a mystery, as I say. In the end, like me, you will be left wondering how to solve this mystery when we cannot accuse anyone of dishonesty without proof.

Can casinos use wired tables, trick wheels, advantages like

that? Is such a thing even possible today? Aren't there sober, upright public commissions who watch the casinos like hawks?

So we're told. And yet we also know that there sometimes is corruption in this world. What remains in the end is this fantastic discrepancy: the systems work so much better at home than in the casinos. But, most intriguingly, there's a strong tendency for the systems to start to work (for real money) when you become "invisible," and keep it secret from the house that you're betting a progression. That's when you learn how to look like a know-nothing instead of a system gambler. The very last words in this book are a reminder to you to *be invisible*, and it's not for nothing that I chose them.

3

Dealing With It

We can't say that some of America's casinos might be using wired tables to rip off high rollers or to short-circuit what would otherwise be winning systems. We have no proof.

What we can do, however, is say just for argument's sake, that a crooked house really could wire the tables to make a good system lose, and then ask what if anything could ever be done about it. To sidestep the wired part, I mean.

That essentially is what this book is all about—not to say some of America's casinos might be using wired tables to keep good mathematical systems from winning, nor to point a finger or accuse anybody of anything, but merely: (1) to present a portfolio of mathematical systems that actually work impressively at your kitchen table, but mysteriously much less effectively in the casinos, and then, (2) to present a different method of playing these same systems, one that hides from the house what you're doing, making you look inconspicuous. Then see what kind of results this new invisibility method produces.

If you can keep it from the house what you're up to, then it becomes irrelevant whether or not wired tables are used to keep successful mathematical systems from paying off. In their eyes you're not a system player, so they'll ignore you!

The secret then would seem to be invisibility. Instead of openly betting a progression, you're going to have to take it a whole dimension higher, to a whole new quantum level of perception. You're going to have a whole bunch of progressions going simultaneously, one for every kind of bet at every kind of table, but you will always and strictly bet *only one bet in each progression per table*. You will be floored at the difference invisibility can make.

The invisibility method means changing tables instead of hanging out at a single table all day. It also means carrying around a tiny notebook to keep track of the last bet made in each of your progressions. But if you can manage that much, then you can make money here, pal, and be in on the ground floor of a great adventure.

II

Craps Systems

4

Half Peak

I first became interested in mathematical gambling systems when I read a magazine article on the subject and began to wonder if it might be possible to supplement my own modest income as a free-lance writer with a little bit extra from the casinos. In particular, the article mentioned a system called Alembert, which fascinated me so thoroughly that I actually got on a bus to Atlantic City to try it out, my first time in a casino ever. It turned out I won $300 that first night playing Alembert, just by simple-mindedly standing at a craps table betting Don't Pass over and over again, but it was an experience I was never again able to duplicate. In hindsight, knowing what I know now, I speculate the pit boss may have sized me up as a newcomer to mathematical gambling systems and tipped off the boxman to let me win a few hundred in the hopes that I'd figure I'd stumbled onto something and come back a week later with larger bills instead of singles. I wasn't as rich as I looked, though, which may have saved me from being victimized, if it *had* been a house with wired tables—or it may have been just dumb luck. Playing a 50–50 bet, I should have won at Alembert roughly 50 percent of the time. When

you try it yourself, in a real casino, you'll see it doesn't work
out that way. Not without your being invisible.

That first night was the beginning of a journey that led to
this book, but not in a straight line by any means. Only two
nights later I lost the $300 playing Alembert again. It seemed
to me at the time that I had hit a run of bad luck. Indeed, to
all outward appearances, that was exactly what happened. My
downfall, I thought, was a mere lack of capital. All I needed
was enough to ride out the bad losing streaks and I'd be all set.
After losing a couple hundred dollars more, this time *my own*
money, I had to stop. I couldn't afford such losses.

Now I am one of these people who happens to believe
there's an invisible God looking in on human affairs and even
getting involved much of the time, so in my case I even went
so far as to imagine my bad luck might be the Lord God
Almighty Himself speaking through events, telling me to back
off here, something's wrong. And so I did. He'd been telling
me a lot of things all along the way, but it wasn't until I'd felt
a little pain that I was ready to listen. What He plainly was saying now was that He wasn't on my side in this one and that I
should stay away from the casinos. It was *not* clear why. It
seemed to me that if I had figured out a way to beat the house
I should be allowed to profit from it. The Almighty, however,
disagreed and only now do I understand why: I would profit
from it all in good time, but evidently more important by far,
from His point of view, was that the story be told. This is
something that might not have happened if I'd been allowed
to milk the system for millions.

From the safety and comfort of my New York City home,
far from the perils and temptations of Atlantic City, I contem-
plated Alembert. It dawned on me then how similar it was to
dollar cost averaging that stock traders utilize and grow rich
on. It was plain enough to me that the underlying principle
had to have some kind of potential, but I couldn't understand
why it should work on the stock exchanges, yet not in the casinos.

Early in my search I discovered drift, a mathematical phenomenon that stems from the fact that losing streaks are always going to be a tiny bit longer than winning streaks, even at an honest table, because the house always wins a tiny bit more often than you do. That in turn causes the amounts of your bets to drift ever higher, thus the term *drift*. I decided drift was the problem and conceived the Half Peak mechanism to compensate for it. (You just close out your progression at *half* your *peak* when a run of good luck carries you that far back down the scale, that's all, then start all over again with a brand-new game all the way back down at your starting point again. More on this later.) But even Half Peak didn't work. It worked on paper and it worked on the kitchen table but it didn't work in the casinos, and the reason was always the same: killer losing streaks that never even gave the Half Peak mechanism a chance to work.

I couldn't figure out what the problem was and once again I lacked the money to continue. A lucky thing for me. In the meantime my study of craps (and then roulette) led me to figure out other systems as well, such as Baby Hardways, Any Craps, Daddy Hardways and others. Once again, they all worked beautifully on paper and on the kitchen table, but not in the casinos, and the explanation was unfailingly the same: bad luck completely beyond what the laws of probability would have predicted, or even believed possible.

I turned to more research. Deeper research. I had done research before but this time I was serious. I went to the New York Public Library and began digging into the major source material in the field. In particular I discovered John Scarne, now deceased, alas, the greatest gambling authority America has ever produced, and there in the back of his masterpiece, *Scarne's Complete Guide to Gambling,* I found a chapter on rigged tables, spelling out the whole technology of it.

It was a revelation. It was from this that I realized there was a genuine possibility there might be wired tables out there.

It was Scarne who taught me about the hitters and missers

at craps, dice that always roll seven and some that never do, how roulette wheels could be rigged, how blackjack and baccarat shoes could be fixed, and all the rest.

Simultaneously I began to hear about how ownership is structured at some of the casinos—stories, for example, that in some places nobody gets to be a pit boss (the guy in the tuxedo who runs the game) without being a part owner of the casino. The pit boss isn't the same as the dealer, mind you. The dealer is merely an employee of the casino. If a button were being pushed it would be the pit boss pushing it. (That's who you want to stay invisible from in the event the house *is* dishonest.)

Later, I read Bernard Baruch's autobiography and learned about his days in the Colorado silver rush as a young man, how he spotted a crooked roulette wheel in one of the casinos, and of his subsequent run-in with the proprietors when he tried to make a little money by always betting the exact opposite of the way the big money was betting. It was Baruch's account that awoke me to the depth of the tradition of crooked gambling equipment in the American (and probably the world) gaming industry, and my realization that not just sleazy houses but even some of the swanky carpet joints might have a crooked table or two. How would you know? How would you even suspect, without coming in with systems that work so well at home?

Later still, I was invited to a neighbor's cookout where I met another guest who told me he once was a bodyguard for one of the big-shot casino executives in Atlantic City, and when he heard the speculation I was entertaining, he told me it was true! In the casino where he worked, he said, underhanded business was in play, in addition to wired tables, but he refused to specify more than wired tables. He even tipped me off that activation can now be done by remote control, à la VCR.

Was he right? Was this a reliable witness? What value should I assign to this man's information?

From this realization that some tables might actually be rigged came the realization that a book should address the conflicting mystery. In the end I decided to do that, to tell the story exactly as it happened, and then present the systems for the reader to try and to note if they work or not. You'll discover they generally do. Then you'll try them in a casino and discover they generally don't. You'll hit phenomenal bad luck, far outside the laws of probability.

How can we explain this? And especially, how can we explain any shift in results if a player tries using the invisibility method and actually gets improved results?

People without power of subpoena can never get firm answers here. On the other hand, if you learn to be invisible and discover that you *do* get improved results, you'll be able to utilize these systems profitably and make money until an aroused public finally forces a full congressional investigation, probably something many years away.

The System Itself

Our first system is Half Peak, which actually is nothing more than Alembert with a single, very helpful modification added: the half-peak mechanism.

The Alembert formula is a pearl of simplicity: every time you win, you decrease your bet by one unit; every time you lose, you increase your bet by one unit. You start anywhere. Pick a number you think is lucky, say 11, and make that your opening bet. If the first bet wins, the second bet is 10. If the first bet loses, the second bet is 12. Then just repeat the process over and over again to infinity.

Consider what happens with every pair of wins and losses. If you bet 11 and lose, then bet 12 and win, you've shelled out $11 + 12 = 23$ but taken in $2 \times 12 = 24$, a profit of exactly one unit. Likewise if you win the first bet, then lose the second, you've rolled out $11 + 10 = 21$, but of course you won $2 \times 11 = 22$ on the first bet, so again the profit is exactly one unit.

That's where the system's profitability comes from. Every pair of wins and losses generates exactly one unit. It doesn't matter if the pair is 11 and 12, 48 and 49, or 16,380 and 16,381, they all generate the same one unit.

The idea behind Alembert is that if you place three hundred bets a night (about 3 to 4 hours' worth in the case of craps, the fastest game), and they work out to be about a 50–50 split between wins and losses (which they generally will be over the long-term average if you learn to be invisible), then you have generated a hundred and fifty additional dollars, wealth that wasn't there before but came into being because of your evening's trading activity. You weren't placing bets, you were buying and selling shares of a company called Pass Line, Inc., on a new kind of stock exchange known as the Craps Table Stock Exchange. Nor does it matter if the wins or losses alternate or if you get long runs of one or the other. It all works out the same. The only requirement is that the wins and losses average out roughly 50–50, which they inevitably do over a long enough period of time. Let's take a look at an example.

Mathematical Analysis
Table 4.1
An Alembert Progression

Bet No.	Amount	Decision	Total Out	Total In	Profit
1	$11	L	$11		−$11
2	12	L	23		−23
3	13	L	36		−36
4	14	W	50	$28	−22
5	13	L	63		−35
6	14	L	77		−49
7	15	W	92	58	−34
8	14	W	106	86	−20
9	13	L	119		−33
10	14	W	133	114	−19

Bet No.	Amount	Decision	Total Out	Total In	Profit
11	13	W	146	140	−6
12	12	L	158		−18
13	13	W	171	166	−5
14	$12	W	$183	$190	$7
(15)	(11)				

Table 4.1 is an account of an actual game of Alembert I played in one of the carpet joints in Atlantic City. I started with a bet of $11 and immediately hit a losing streak, losing five of my first six bets. At its worst, I was $49 in the hole, and yet look what happened. Out of fourteen bets overall, I won seven, lost seven, and ended up with a net profit of precisely $7, or one-half unit per bet. I won and lost the same number of bets, yet ended up with a clear, solid profit. Moreover, it would all have worked out exactly the same even if the wins and losses had all been reversed. Look at table 4.2, please.

Table 4.2
A Mirror Image of Table 4.1

Bet No.	Amount	Decision	Total Out	Total In	Profit
1	$11	W	$11	$22	$11
2	10	W	21	42	21
3	9	W	30	60	30
4	8	L	38		22
5	9	W	47	78	31
6	8	W	55	94	39
7	7	L	62		32
8	8	L	70		24
9	9	W	79	112	33
10	8	L	87		25
11	9	L	96		16
12	10	W	106	$132	26
13	9	L	115		17
14	$10	L	$125		$7
(15)	(11)				

This is a purely hypothetical Alembert game, exactly the opposite of the real-life game in table 4.1, devised purely to illustrate that I would have won exactly the same $7 even if I had lost all the bets I actually won and won all the bets I actually lost. If you look at it as a balance sheet, table 4.2 seems to be a much more successful game than table 4.1 because the severe losing streak at the beginning of table 4.1 becomes a fabulous winning streak at the beginning of table 4.2. And yet they both finish the same, with a profit of one-half unit per bet.

Alembert looks like a great system up close, and it is, one of the best of the traditional systems, but unfortunately it has two very serious problems.

The immediate problem is that you must have enough capital on hand to be able to bankroll a bad losing streak. Theory says it doesn't matter even if you lose so much that your bets eventually rise as high as a hundred units or more. Sooner or later your luck will change, and when it does you'll be winning a hundred units or more per bet, all the way back down the scale to where you started from, and in the end you'll net one unit for every two bets placed. The problem is bankrolling such a progression, assuming you get one so ghastly, and you could. People do. Running your bets up from eleven units all the way to a hundred units is going to cost you somewhere in the neighborhood of five thousand units, or $5,000 if you use $1 betting units. Which brings us early on to one of the cardinal principles of all mathematical gambling systems: *keep your betting units small.* We touched on this earlier, but now you must consider it earnestly. It's bad enough to have to live with the possibility of a crooked house gunning for you with their possibly-wired tables, but don't go making it worse by mismanaging your capital. Increase and decrease by $1 increments only, not $2, $3, or $5 increments. Otherwise the amount of capital required will break you the very first time you hit a serious losing streak. This *apart* from the possibility of the tables being rigged.

Consider this: the cold, raw mathematics of the Law of Probability is that once a week or so, on average, you're going to hit a losing streak of nine in a row. *Even if they're not juicing the tables on you.* Every two weeks, ten in a row. Once a year, on average, you're going to have to eat *fifteen* in a row, *even if you're 100 percent successful in staying invisible.* All this can float the amounts of your bets up into the stratosphere absolutely effortlessly, and heaven help you if you started with too large a betting unit, so be realistic.

Now what about Half Peak? Where does this mathematical device Half Peak come in?

As you may recall, I said Alembert had *two* very serious problems. Having enough capital was only one of them. The other problem is *drift,* another honest mathematical phenomenon that stems from the fact that over the long run the house is always going to win a tiny bit more often than you. It has nothing to do with a crooked house cheating you in this case. Drift will happen in an honest casino. It's just in the nature of any game where the house has that built-in mathematical edge.

According to probability theory, a casino wins 507 out of every 1,000 bets and you win 493, on average. This in itself would be no problem: the one unit profit from every two bets can easily cover the cost of these 14 losses in a hypothetical run of 1,000 bets which produces a hypothetical $500 of profit. But because the house always wins a tiny bit more often than you do, even at an honest table, your losing streaks are always going to be a tiny bit longer than your winning streaks, which means the amounts of your bets will tend inevitably to get higher and higher as the tide of luck ebbs and flows. Thus if you were to open a game of Alembert with a bet of 50 units, in the first hour your bets might work their way up and down to, say, a high of 60 and a low of 40, but in the second hour they would have a disturbing tendency to be something more like 64 and 44. And in the third hour they could be even higher than that. After a few days you'd find your bets averaging around a hundred or so, and fifty would be a number you'd be lucky to see, if ever.

Obviously your progression has to have some way to correct for drift or you find yourself betting hundreds of units on every bet and see all your profits absorbed in financing these enormous bets, not to mention how obvious it would be to the house, and what it would do to your all-important invisibility.

The way to correct is to end your Alembert progression at *Half* your *Peak* when a winning streak finally carries you that far back down the scale, then start all over again with a brand-new game.

Now as a practical matter you aren't going to open a game of Half Peak with a bet of $50 because a hairy losing streak early on could send your bets up to $80 or $90 very quickly and soak up thousands of dollars of your capital, and you would have no guarantee that another hairy losing streak wasn't just around the corner. Double whammies like that could clean out the Emir of Kuwait, *and these things do happen.* A more reasonable game would begin with a bet of, say, $10 or $12, depending on what the house minimum is. You want to be at least seven units above the house minimum in order to be able to store up your good luck if it comes early on. A typical minimum is $5. If you shop around you might be able to find a minimum of $3, especially in the weekday mornings and afternoons when traffic is light, but beware of going to the casinos when traffic is light. Invisibility requires you to get lost in a crowd, remember, so always take care never to go to the tables except when it's as crowded as Times Square on New Year's Eve. Remember—once they get to know your face, you're no longer invisible.

So you begin your game of Half Peak on a bet of $10. By and by drift will carry your progression up to a peak which is more than double your opening bet. If you're lucky enough to work your way back down to half that peak, whatever it is, you quit and start a new game at $10.

For example, if you work your way up to a peak of $30, then half peak is $15; you quit as soon as you work your way back down to $15 and no further—game over, victory claimed. Then you start a fresh game at $10. You've corrected for drift by jumping $5 down the scale, from $15 to $10, a minor loss that you cheerfully accept as part of the cost of doing business, knowing it has saved you from the mathematical gangrene of drift.

Whatever your peak turns out to be, you quit as soon as you work your way back down to half of it. Even if bad luck carries your progression as high as $50, you quit as soon as you get back down to $25, then start a fresh game at $10. But you should get back down to half peak again sooner or later. You practically always will on your kitchen table.

And that's it. That's how Half Peak is played. Your first system. And it works. And how. Wait'll you try it on your kitchen table. You're not gonna believe it even after you've seen it with your own eyes.

The bets for playing Half Peak at craps are called the "Pass Line" and the "Don't Pass" line. They're there in fig. 4.1, the Craps Layout, the pair of parallel stripes running along the length of both edges of the green felt and curving up both ends of the table. They're the even-money bets, the ones you play Half Peak with. Think of these two bets as your introduction to the Craps Layout. If you place your chips on the Pass Line, you're betting on the shooter to win. If you place your chips on the Don't Pass line, you're betting him to lose. Either way it's a 1-to-1 payoff. If, for example, you bet $5 and win, the dealer gives you back your $5 plus $5 from the house. If you lose, the house keeps your $5. That's all. (The actual rules of craps, for future reference, are as follows: a first throw of 7 or 11 wins, a first throw of 2, 3 or 12 loses, and a first throw of 4, 5, 6, 8, 9 or 10 can be won only by repeating the number thrown before a seven appears.)

A Frank Evaluation

Half Peak is a good introductory system. The pace is comfortably slow and it has the advantage of teaching you the rules of

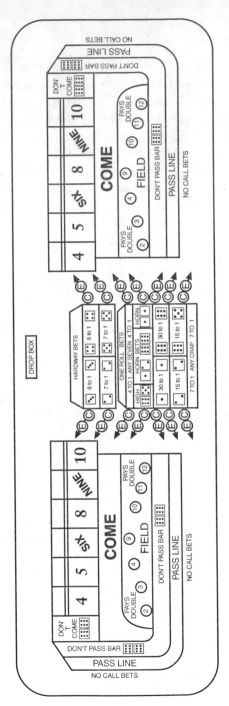

The Craps Layout

craps quickly and painlessly. In an actual casino you'll be playing Half Peak side-by-side with several other craps progressions, getting down one bet in each progression per table, all for the purpose of being discreet about betting progressively instead of randomly.

Half Peak is also a fine roulette game. When you get into playing roulette, once again you'll have several progressions going at once and you'll bet the next bet in each of them at each new wheel. In this case you'll be running separate Half Peak progressions on every 1-to-1 bet on the roulette layout: red, black, odd, even, high, low, but again, only one bet in each progression per wheel. Pick a crowded wheel. The harder it is for you to get a place at the table, the more suitable the table is for invisibility.

Blackjack and Baccarat players will find Half Peak very well suited to those two highly popular card games. According to Scarne, card games are every bit as rigable as any of the other games in a dishonest casino. Here the shoe that the dealer deals the cards from could be rigged, say by a second hidden slot just above the slot where the cards come out, recessed so your eyes can't see it. Anytime a dealer needs an ace (or any other card) he can slide it out. To beat the house at Blackjack and Baccarat, one must learn to be as invisible as when playing craps or roulette. Thus, you can bet only one bet in a progression per table, which means it's going to be a very slow game. You make up for this by using $5 or $10 betting units. This is risky, though, so you must set limits. At the first Blackjack table you bet, say, $20 —then change tables regardless of whether you win or lose. If you win, bet $15 the next time you sit down. If you lose, bet $25 the next time you sit down. With $5 or $10 betting units it doesn't look to the dealer or boxperson that your lone, seemingly random bet is part of an ongoing progression.

Baccarat's the same, only baccarat also offers an 8-to-1 Tie that you can build a nice progression on. (More on this later when we get to the long-shot bets.) Use $10 betting units on the 1-to-1 Bankers/Players, $5 betting units on the 8-to-1 Tie, and place only one bet in each of your progressions per table once again so no one ever realizes your overall betting is organized progressively and not random at all.

What's going to happen, when you finally get it *totally* together, is that you're going to walk around town with a tiny notebook, recording the next bet in each of every possible kind of progression in every available kind of casino game, and quietly hit every casino in town systematically, discreetly placing, for example, only one bet in each of your baccarat progressions when you're in the baccarat section, roulette progressions when you're in the roulette section, and so on, all across the city the whole day long. If you keep the notebook hidden and stick to busy, busy days, no one will ever know.

Homework

Here's your fun homework assignment for this chapter, not only easy but lots of pleasure as well: get yourself a pocketful of quarters, dimes, nickels and pennies and play a game of Half Peak on your kitchen table just to see for yourself how the system works out. You could use any 1–1 bet. It doesn't have to be craps. If you have a toy roulette wheel, try any of the 1 to 1's. Use pennies to represent $1 chips, nickels to represent $5 chips, etc. Budget $50 for yourself and $50 for the house to simulate $5,000 capital each.

See who cleans out whom.

No, you don't have to get together $100 in cash to run this test, just use IOU's. Your actual cash need here is probably no more than $3 or $5 worth of laundry change, but please be accurate with the IOU's so that if by some miracle you should just happen to break the house, you'll know you really did it.

This is a fundamental exercise. Its purpose is not so much to teach you Half Peak as to awaken you to the realization that the systems in this book actually do work.

5

Baby Hardways

What a revelation it would be if any well-known casino has been using rigged tables and kept it secret all this time! If it's actually so, how would it be exposed?

That's an interesting question. My guess is that if it *is* so, some Capitol Hill politician would be the one to bust it open. It's a fine way for an up-and-coming young voice to become known and heard across the land. It also has the advantage of diverting public attention from an administration's troubles, which in turn would surely win that administration's warm support. Also, it would be a huge vote-getter. Millions of people will ponder if they may have been cheated by a casino and demand some answers. So it will probably be a politician rather than an ambitious prosecutor who will uncover whatever truth is hidden, but don't be too quick to minimize the ruckus that a good prosecutor can raise. It wouldn't even have to be a Federal case. A local prosecutor can raise holy hell if it turns out he's sunk his claws into something genuinely criminal, a certainty if he actually located a casino using wired tables. In any case, it would have to be somebody with power of subpoena, such as a congressperson or prosecutor. A media reporter would run into a stone wall and that would be that. Whoever the investigators turn out to be, they might consider getting in touch with Gamblers Anonymous to share their intelligence.

Where would they begin? Disgruntled ex-employees are a gold mine of information in situations of this sort, but the wisest approach might be directed toward the upstream end of it, setting aside casinos and inquiring into equipment manufacturers. Who might be manufacturing dishonest gaming equipment today and who are their customers? A quick look at a customer list could save months of inquiry, asking casino employees what they know or observe.

Now of course the manufacturers of any dishonest equipment will see all of this coming miles away.

Will such people tamper with their records and commit perjury to keep the truth from the public? Perjury is a serious crime. Manufacturing crooked equipment, on the other hand, is probably no crime at all, since the manufacturer wouldn't be defrauding *his* customers. Would a manufacturer who has committed no actual crime risk the penalties for perjury in order to save his dishonest customers' hides? It's complicated. And it would probably depend on how much money is at stake. That's what usually decides these kinds of things.

I say the upstream way would be the way to go. One would start with the manufacturers. Who, if anyone, is producing crooked wheels, tables, dice, devices? For whose use? Once an investigation gets that far, the rest will suggest itself automatically and the whole matter will fall to hand very neatly. Probably there will even be a few of my own readers who'll be moved to prod their congressperson to action, once they see that the systems that prove themselves at home somehow don't work in the casinos.

The System Itself

Baby Hardways, our second mathematical system, is one of the simplest of the high-leverage gambling systems, those based on the various long shots and requiring more capital to back up.

It's based on a technique that parallels to some extent a trading technique in the stock market known as "short selling." Basically what happens is that a slick operator sees a company that is overpriced—the public has temporarily bid up the price unrealistically high for some reason—and so he borrows somebody else's shares of that company in order to sell them while the price is high. Then he returns the same number of shares later on, buying new ones after the share price has fallen back down to a realistic level. The difference between the unrealistic price and the realistic price is his profit. That's assuming he guessed right and the price goes back down. But sometimes he guesses wrong and the price goes higher still. In fact, lots of the time he guesses wrong and the price goes higher still, but this is no problem because a good market operator just borrows even more shares to sell, now that the price is higher still, and thus makes even more profit on an even wider spread. If the share price fools him again and rises still higher, he borrows vastly more shares, and makes vastly more money from the vastly wider spread when the share prices finally return to reality. As always, the bastard makes money no matter what, assuming he has enough reserve capital to see him through a bad losing streak, which a good operator always does. The pros on the stock exchange know to keep their betting units small. You don't have to tell *them*.

Baby Hardways parallels this short-selling maneuver at the Craps table. It's much riskier than Half Peak because it's a 7-to-1 long shot, not a 1-to-1 even-money bet, which means your chances of wipeout are much greater, but it's more profitable, assuming you don't wipe out. The short-seller on the floor of the stock exchange doesn't have to worry about the possibility of a crooked casino wiring the tables on him, but you do. That much said, I can't remind you often enough how helpful it is for a mathematical system player to stay invisible.

Anyway, back to business. Mathematically the Baby Hardways system is blessedly simple and straightforward. Begin by looking at fig. 5.1, please, the Center of the Craps Layout.

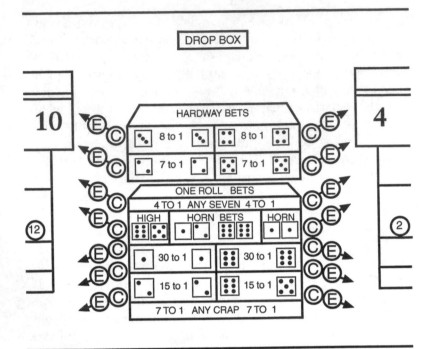

Fig. 5.1. The Center of the Craps Layout

This is a veritable supermarket when it comes to wagers. There's an astounding variety of bets that can be found on the layout, but not all of them are terrific bets, and some of them are absolute dogs. The worst ones are the one-roll proposition bets on either a 2 or 12. They pay only 30 to 1, but their true odds are 35 to 1, which means that the house is taking an extraordinarily large bite on those two. A fair payoff ought to be 34 to 1. This isn't to say you shouldn't bet them if you get a strong hunch—quite the contrary, betting random hunches helps you to stay invisible—but only to say you shouldn't try to base a mathematical system on the 2 or 12. No system could ever wring a profit out of them. In chapter 17 we'll learn about a roulette system called Lucky Number that takes on the 35-

to-1 ultra long-shot on the roulette table, but in Lucky Number those 35-to-1 odds are against true odds of only 36 or 37 to 1 (depending on whether it's a single- or double-zero wheel). With that narrow a spread you can work all kinds of number systems, but a 30-to-1 payoff against a true 35 to 1 is just too much of a gap to overcome safely except, as I say, when you're betting one random hunch, both to test your luck and to help obscure your progressions from the house.

This is a little like being a commando, all this invisibility and sneaking around behind enemy lines. Do you have the emotional stamina to be one? Being a mathematician and a capitalist isn't enough. You must also be at least partly commando.

The other conspicuous loser on the Craps layout is the "Field." You'll see it there in fig. 4.1, the Craps Layout, looming large over both ends of the table—large, because the house is hoping you'll equate largeness with goodness and go for it which, once again, is all right to do as long as you're doing it either on a hunch or for invisibility's sake. Don't take it seriously as a mathematical opportunity because it certainly is nothing of the sort.

The Field is probably the single most profitable bet the house has on the craps layout (profitable for the house, I mean), not because the house's bite is larger than with the 30-to-1 deuce or twelve—it isn't—but because so many people who don't understand the underlying mathematics see the Field, think it's a good deal, and go for it. The house is telling you, in effect, that there are only eleven possible numbers that can be rolled, 2, 3, 4, 5, 6, 7, 8, 9, 10, 11 and 12, which is true, and that if a 2, 3, 4, 9, 10, 11 or 12 is rolled, seven of the eleven possible numbers, it will pay you 1-to-1 even money (except 2 or 12, which pays double), same as Pass or Don't Pass. On the face of it, it seems like a reasonable offer but the catch is that the seven numbers they pay off on are the seven numbers which appear *least* often, while the four numbers they don't pay off on are the four numbers which appear *most* often. Have a look at table 5.1, please, the Dice Paradigm.

Table 5.1
The Dice Paradigm

Die 1 + Die 2 =

1 + 1 = 2	3 + 1 = 4	5 + 1 = 6
1 + 2 = 3	3 + 2 = 5	5 + 2 = 7
1 + 3 = 4	3 + 3 = 6	5 + 3 = 8
1 + 4 = 5	3 + 4 = 7	5 + 4 = 9
1 + 5 = 6	3 + 5 = 8	5 + 5 = 10
1 + 6 = 7	3 + 6 = 9	5 + 6 = 11
2 + 1 = 3	4 + 1 = 5	6 + 1 = 7
2 + 2 = 4	4 + 2 = 6	6 + 2 = 8
2 + 3 = 5	4 + 3 = 7	6 + 3 = 9
2 + 4 = 6	4 + 4 = 8	6 + 4 = 10
2 + 5 = 7	4 + 5 = 9	6 + 5 = 11
2 + 6 = 8	4 + 6 = 10	6 + 5 = 12

SUMMARY

1 combination equals 2
2 combinations equal 3
3 combinations equal 4
4 combinations equal 5
5 combinations equal 6
6 combinations equal 7
5 combinations equal 8
4 combinations equal 9
3 combinations equal 10
2 combinations equal 11
1 combination equals 12

This isn't as complicated as it looks. What you're looking at is a chart of the 36 possible combinations that can be rolled with two dice of six sides each. When we view the possibilities in this light it becomes obvious why the Field is a sucker bet: of the 36 possibilities, the seven payoff numbers account for only *16* of them, while the four numbers that don't pay off—5, 6, 7 and 8—account for a full *20* of the 36 possibilities.

Thus, what the house is really offering you with the Field is a payoff of 1 to 1 against true odds of 16 to 20. You've got the 16, they've got the 20. This is plainly no mathematical opportunity at all. For every 36 Field bets made you can statistically expect to win only 16, and lose 20.

The casinos themselves realize what an abysmal deal this is and to try to sweeten it they offer to pay *double* if a 2 or 12 is rolled. At one house in Atlantic City, they even offer to pay *triple* on the Field if a 12 is rolled, but even with this the Field is a poor choice compared with Pass or Don't Pass. The Field is useful only for invisibility's sake, for betting occasional random bets to help obscure the fact that you're intermittently betting killer progressions. On a less-than-crowded day this kind of thing can do it. Now perhaps you're beginning to get a feel for the kind of harmony and interconnectedness that true invisibility entails. You'll see. You'll get there and you'll learn fast. Profit will move you.

Anyway, getting back to Baby Hardways, in fig. 5.1, the Center of the Craps Layout, we see at top center, in capital letters, the words HARDWAY BETS, and underneath them a sublayout of four bets, one of them a pair of 2's, offering 7 to 1, followed by a pair of 3's, at 9 to 1, a pair of 4's at 9 to 1, and finally a pair of 5's at 7 to 1 again—all the doubles, in other words, except a pair of 1's and a pair of 6's, the 2 and the 12, which come only one way and therefore have no hardways.

But what do we mean by "hardway," anyway? What is a hard way? "Hard," in this case, means difficult. Look again at table 5.1, the Dice Paradigm. There are, for example, three different ways to throw a 4: 3-1, 2-2 and 1-3. Only one of the three ways is a pair of 2's. It's the most difficult kind of 4 to roll, and therefore it's called the "hard" 4. When you bet a hard 4, you're betting a pair of 2's will be rolled before a seven, or any other four. (The other fours—3-1 and 1-3—are called "easy 4.")

It's like a grab bag with 36 numbers inside. Eight of them (six 7's and two easy 4's) will make you lose and one of them (hard 4) will make you win. Eight to one, in other words. The other 27 possibilities are neutral. If you're betting, say, hard 4, the only numbers that are of any concern to you are 4's and 7's, all of which make you lose except the pair of 2's, the hard 4 which, when it comes, pays 7 to 1 against true odds of 8 to 1, a very sweet payoff, pal, wait'll it happens to you, you'll like it just fine. Likewise the hard 10, or in layman's language, a pair of 5's. It too is a 7-to-1 payoff against true odds of 8 to 1.

In fact, there are two different kinds of hardways, mathematically. The hard 4 and hard 10 are one kind, and the hard 6 and hard 8 are another kind, a harsher, riskier 9-to-1 payout against true 10 to 1 odds. The actual figures favor hard 6 and hard 8, the house has a narrower edge on those two, 10 percent versus 12.5 percent.

The Baby Hardways system works as follows: you bet one unit on either hard 4 or hard 10. Mathematically they're both the same. Since these are long shots, not 1 to 1, the house will let you bet as little as $1. The same with all the long shots. If you lose, which you probably will, it being a true 8 to 1, you increase your bet to two units, then three, then four, etc., as in Half Peak, until you finally win. Then, instead of decreasing the bet by one unit, as in Half Peak, you decrease it by ten units—eight because it's a true 8 to 1, *plus two extra units in order to create the all-important drift downward.* Once you've created the drift downward, the amounts of your bets, over time, will always tend to drift toward zero, rather than upward. As always, it's just a matter of having enough capital on hand to be able to ride out any nasty losing streaks, which, bad as they are on the 1-to-1 bets, are pitilessly worse on the 8-to-1 bets.

On Hard 6 and Hard 8 it's exactly the same except that when you win you correct by $12, not $10. The reason is that Hard 6 and Hard 8 are true *10*-to-1 shots, not 8-to-1 shots, so you must correct by *$10*, not $8, plus once again an additional $2 to create the all-important drift downward.

In a theoretically perfect game it's immediately clear why Baby Hardways is so profitable: if it takes exactly nine turns to win, you've shelled out $1 + $2 + $3 + ... + $9 = $45, but you've won back 7 × $9 = $63 plus your $9 bet, or $72 in all, making for a tidy profit of $27.

But even when it's not theoretically perfect it works out very nicely, as you'll quickly see when you start trying it on your kitchen table. The trick, of course, is to make it work in a casino. Why should it be harder to make it work in a casino? Why should it be necessary always to be invisible? Heaven willing, this may one day soon be a widely studied question.

Mathematical Analysis

The mathematical analysis of 8-to-1 Baby Hardways is in the next chapter where we compare and contrast it with the 10-to-1 Daddy Hardways, its mathematical cousin.

A Frank Evaluation

Baby Hardways is going to be two more profit centers for you as you stroll around town with that secret little notebook of yours. It's a marvelous system, and you'll be running two Baby Hardways progressions at once, one on the Hard 4 and one on the Hard 10. As always, you'll place only one bet in each progression per table, then change tables for invisibility's sake. You've already got four profitable progressions going for you here—Pass Line, Don't Pass, Hard 4 and Hard 10—and you aren't even into your third system yet.

Learn them all. That's what it's really going to come down to in the end. There, on your kitchen table, become fluent with *all* the systems, then play them all simultaneously, taking care always to simulate betting random bets here and there and just changing tables a lot, as gamblers often do. (Actually, if you're doing it right, no one will even notice you, much less notice any special pattern of travel between tables.)

The idea is to look like a know-nothing. The closer you can get to projecting that, the better. The one thing you don't want to look like is a predator. Don't enter the casino with a gleam in your eye, unless it's the simpleton kind of gleam. Try to look like an overfed calf. That's the right kind of look. Your chances of making money may go up if you can manage that. Look like exactly what you want them to believe you are.

By the way, the Baby Hardways formula also works on the so-called "numbers" game, the illegal gambling game found in most major cities in the United States, only not as well since the numbers people offer a lousy payoff compared to the casinos. The other main hitch, apart from the lousy deal itself, is that you can only get in one bet a day, making it a slow, slow game, more like watching the grass grow, although it can still turn a profit if you can figure out how to stay invisible, say by having different people place the successive bets. Here, of course, you don't place your bet in a casino but in your local numbers parlor. I can't even begin to tell you where it is, you'll just have to ask around. You're gonna meet some real fine people there, wait'll you see.

In its most popular form the numbers game is played on the so-called "Brooklyn number," which is the last three digits of the total parimutuel take at the local racetrack the previous day, a number supposedly impossible to predict or rig (hah!), easily accessible to everyone just by looking at the morning paper. The number itself has nothing at all to do with Brooklyn. I don't know why it's called the Brooklyn number. It didn't start in Brooklyn, it started in Harlem, but somehow it has come to be called the Brooklyn number throughout the country.

In the numbers game you can bet three numbers, two numbers or one number. If you're betting three numbers you're guessing the last three digits of the racetrack take exactly—a

999-to-1 shot. The payoff, in New York City at least, is 650 to 1, making it a consummate sucker bet. Likewise, if you bet two numbers, you're trying to guess the *first two* digits of the Brooklyn number, the hundreds column and the tens column. The true odds are 99 to 1, but the payoff is only 75 to 1— another sucker bet.

A single number bet at numbers is also a sucker bet, paying only 7 to 1 on a true 9 to 1 (what the numbers people call "8 *for* 1," which means you get $8 for your $1, only you don't get your $1 back, the parlor keeps it), but you can still build a minimally profitable progression on a single number bet. The way to do it is to correct by $11 after every win, $9 to match the true 9 to 1, plus an extra $2 to create the all-important drift downward. This will win at the numbers game, although not terrifically so.

Your real problem in a numbers parlor isn't that the game they're offering you is a lousy one, although it certainly is, and that certainly is a problem, but that if you start winning regularly they may wise on to you and bounce you from their parlor violently. Don't underestimate the potential on this one. Like all the other kinds of bad luck, it too can happen. If you get any indication that it's on the verge of happening, I urge you to take their word for it and leave peacefully. Don't try to tell them about your rights. Breaking bones also is part of their business. They will show you if you insist.

Homework

Here's your homework assignment for this chapter: no, not to play a game of Baby Hardways, although you can if you want to, but merely to pick a Hardway of your own, Hard 4, say, a pair of 2's, and roll the dice to see how often your Hardway comes up, if it really does so about once in every thirty-six rolls, as the Law of Probability stipulates.

After verifying that the Law of Probability is right, continue rolling the dice to discover the longest time you can go *without* the Hardway coming up. Set aside a full hour and note the longest losing streak you'll experience in that time.

You'll find it's *much* longer than you expected. Serious food for thought.

6

Daddy Hardways

Where does the short seller's profit come from? Does it relate to what an unprincipled casino would be doing? This is an interesting question and one well worth asking. Both of them are making money by taking advantage of the ignorance of some sucker. Is it therefore the same?

The answer is no, and the reason is that it's not a matter of being taken advantage of so much as a matter of being *dishonestly* taken advantage of. That's the difference, that key word *dishonestly*. The short seller is taking advantage of the ignorance of the person who buys a stock for more than its worth, but it's an honest strategy. No one's deceiving anyone. The buyer has access to the same information as the rest of the public. He forms his own opinion of what the stock is worth and if his opinion is wrong it's not the seller's doing.

With the casino it would be different, it *would* be their doing. A casino without scruples would be defrauding people. That's the difference, the fraud. The deceit. The duplicity. Not that one guy knows what the stock's really worth and the other guy doesn't as in short selling, but that one guy would be deliberately deceiving the other.

40 CRAPS SYSTEMS

(Is it right for a short seller to take undue advantage? It is as long as the situation is honest, as long as nobody's lying to anybody about what's going on. The put-upon customer could have reasons of his own for being willing to pay the higher price.)

The System Itself

Daddy Hardways is just like Baby Hardways, only it's played on the 10-to-1 Hard 6 and Hard 8 bets instead of the 8-to-1 Hard 4 and Hard 10 bets. Once again you've got a grab bag with 36 numbers inside. *Ten* of them (six 7's and four easy 6's) make you lose and one of them (Hard 6) makes you win. That's when you're playing Hard 6. With Hard 8 the four easy 8's (and the 7) make you lose and the Hard 8 makes you win.

The important thing here is getting a feel for the distinction between the two kinds of Hardways, Baby and Daddy. What really is the difference between an 8 to 1 and a 10 to 1?

Mathematical Analysis

Table 6.1
Baby Hardways—*Hard 4*

BET NO.	AMOUNT	DECISION	TOTAL OUT	TOTAL IN	PROFIT
1	$1	L	$1		-$1
2	2	L	3		-3
3	3	L	6		-6
4	4	L	10		-10
5	5	L	15		-15
6	6	L	21		-21
7	7	L	28		-28
8	8	L	36		-36
9	9	L	45		-45
10	10	L	55		-55
11	11	L	66		-66
12	12	L	78		-78

Bet No.	Amount	Decision	Total Out	Total In	Profit
13	13	L	91		−91
14	14	L	105		−105
15	15	L	120		−120
16	16	L	136		−136
17	17	L	153		−153
18	18	W	171	$144	−27
19	8	L	179		−35
20	9	L	188		−44
21	10	L	198		−54
22	11	L	209		−65
23	12	L	221		−77
24	13	L	234		−90
25	14	L	248		−104
26	15	W	263	264	1
27	5	L	268		−4
28	6	L	274		−10
29	7	W	281	320	39
30	1	L	282		38
31	2	L	284		36
32	3	L	287		33
33	4	W	291	352	61
34	1	L	292		60
35	2	W	294	368	74
36	1	L	295		73
37	2	L	297		71
38	3	W	300	392	92
39	1	L	301		91
40	2	L	303		89
41	3	L	306		86
42	4	L	310		82
43	5	L	315		77
44	6	W	321	440	119
45	1	L	322		118
46	2	L	324		116
47	3	L	327		113
48	4	L	331		109
49	5	L	336		104
50	6	L	342		98
51	7	W	349	496	147
52	1	L	350		146
53	2	L	352		144
54	3	L	355		141
55	4	L	359		137

Bet No.	Amount	Decision	Total Out	Total In	Profit
56	5	L	364		132
57	6	L	370		126
58	7	L	377		119
59	8	L	385		111
60	$9	W	$394	$568	$174
61	(1)				

In tables 6.1 and 6.2 we see two different Baby Hardways games, the first played on the Hard 4 with the gentler 8-to-1 odds and the second played on the Hard 6 with the rougher 10-to-1 odds. Definite contrasts appear when we compare the two.

Look at the highs and lows, for example—the extremes. In table 6.1 the game played on Hard 4 has a high of $174 (Bet No. 60) and a low of –$153 (Bet No. 17). The game in table 6.2, on the other hand, has a high of $200 (Bet No. 57) and a low of -$223 (Bet No. 26). You can immediately see how much greater the capital requirements are for playing a 10 to 1 rather than an 8 to 1. The game on the 10 to 1 went a full –$223 into the hole. The game on the 8 to 1 went in only –$153. *The 10 to 1 required roughly half again as much capital as the 8 to 1.*

Now you will say that no game is ever typical and that certainly is true, but the generalities apply and should be respected. As the odds lengthen, the risk increases faster than the payoff. This is a reliable rule of thumb and a worthy meditation target.

Table 6.2
Baby Hardways—*Hard 6*

Bet No.	Amount	Decision	Total Out	Total In	Profit
1	$1	L	$1		–$1
2	2	L	3		–3

Bet No.	Amount	Decision	Total Out	Total In	Profit
3	3	L	6		−6
4	4	W	10	$40	30
5	1	L	11		29
6	2	L	13		27
7	3	L	16		24
8	4	L	20		20
9	5	L	25		15
10	6	L	31		9
11	7	L	38		2
12	8	L	46		−6
13	9	L	55		−15
14	10	L	65		−25
15	11	L	76		−36
16	12	L	88		−48
17	13	L	101		−61
18	14	L	115		−75
19	15	L	130		−90
20	16	L	146		−106
21	17	L	163		−123
22	18	L	181		−141
23	19	L	200		−160
24	20	L	220		−180
25	21	L	241		−201
26	22	L	263		−223
27	23	W	286	270	−16
28	11	L	297		−27
29	12	W	309	390	81
30	1	L	310		80
31	2	L	312		78
32	3	L	315		75
33	4	L	319		71
34	5	L	324		66
35	6	L	330		60
36	7	L	337		53
37	8	L	345		45
38	9	L	354		36
39	10	L	364		26
40	11	L	375		15
41	12	L	387		3
42	13	L	400		−10
43	14	L	414		−24
44	15	W	429	540	111
45	3	L	432		108
46	4	L	436		104

BET No.	AMOUNT	DECISION	TOTAL OUT	TOTAL IN	PROFIT
47	5	L	441		99
48	6	L	447		93
49	7	W	454	610	156
50	1	L	455		155
51	2	L	457		153
52	3	L	460		150
53	4	L	464		146
54	5	L	469		141
55	6	L	475		135
56	7	L	482		128
57	$8	W	$490	$690	$200
58	(1)				

Also, look at the lengths of the losing streaks, please, another key point. The 8 to 1's longest losing streak was 17 in a row (Bet Nos. 1–17, inclusive) while the 10 to 1's longest losing streak was 22 in a row (Bet Nos. 5–26, inclusive). Plus: the 8 to 1's second-longest losing streak was only 8 in a row (Bet Nos. 52–59, inclusive) while the 10 to 1's second-longest losing streak was *14* in a row (Bet Nos. 30–43, inclusive), almost double.

In chapter 4 I had you simulate $5,000 capital to test out Half Peak which is a mere 1 to 1. How much more capital would it take to simulate Baby Hardways, which is 7 to 1, or Daddy Hardways, which is 9 to 1? Too much. Much too much. In actual practice you're not going to be able to play Baby Hardways the way you played Half Peak, where you commit a large pool of capital. You'd be too likely to lose it all on your first serious unlucky streak, irrespective of the possibility of a house trying to cheat you. Instead, you have to set limits on how deeply in you're willing to go. I'd recommend $220 (enough for $1 through $20, inclusive), *max*. Or if you're really sporty, maybe $335 (enough for $1 through $25, inclusive), but certainly not much more than that. It makes more sense just to set a strict limit and swallow your losses if you hit an unlucky streak (or are perhaps being conned very skillfully by

a dishonest house), rather than plunge yourself into bankruptcy out of commitment to some mathematical progression. On
Wall Street this is called using your brain. It has its place in
the casino as well. I specified $5,000 for Half Peak but I won't
specify *any* amount for the long shots because the long shots
are just too risky. The only sane way to deal with the long shots
is to decide on some reasonable limit and then stick to your
decision.

A Frank Evaluation

Daddy Hardways is risky but it's also *very* profitable, wait'll
you see. It's the most lush by far of all the systems we've
looked at up to this point. It's going to account for yet two
more progressions in that secret little notebook of yours, this
time the Hard 6 and the Hard 8.

At first practice with Baby and Daddy Hardways and let
your bets float all the way up to $100 or more, if need be, just
to see how profitable these two systems actually are; but when
it comes time to start practicing for an actual trip to a casino,
limit your bets to $20 on both kinds of Hardways, $25 or $30
max, because otherwise they can swallow you up alive. As soon
as your progression leads you to bet $20 and you lose, forget
it. Start all over again at zero. It becomes too obvious to the
house what you're up to otherwise—and you won't be invisible
anymore, in addition to the unreasonable financial risk.

With respect to the illegal urban numbers' game (leaving the
casinos for a moment and returning to the sleazy urban numbers parlors), there actually is a way to beat the numbers parlor, but I'm afraid to suggest it for fear it might get you a bullet in the head. Your heirs will sue me for product liability.
Still, the concept is too interesting not to discuss.

You will recall that at the numbers game the single-number
bet has true odds of 9 to 1 and pays 7 to 1. Since there are
only ten possible single-number bets—0 through 9 inclusive—

it's easy to run ten separate progressions on each of the ten possible numbers simultaneously. Remember that with the numbers game there's only one bet per day on each of the ten numbers. With a pace as slow as that, anyone can keep track of the ten simultaneous progressions.

Also, since you're covering every possible number at once, you always have a winner *every day*. The guys who run the parlor are really going to love this.

That's the math of it. In actual practice you'll have to manage it like a good covert operations officer and get ten separate people to place the bets, all feigning no connection whatsoever with one another, all swapping numbers with each other every day so nobody ever appears to be betting a progression, everybody always appears to be betting randomly, but even then the hoods'll quickly pick up on the fact that something's going on, I can all but guarantee it. If nothing else they'll surely pick up on the fact that they're suddenly facing a heavy payout every single day of the week, no matter what. That alone could get you a bullet in the brain. It might be better just to have your trusted henchmen do the betting and you keep away from the parlor altogether. I pass along these ideas concerning the numbers racket partly to make this book more colorful and interesting and partly to give you some sense of the larger scope that mathematical gambling systems can take in, but as for actually trying to burn the hoods at the numbers parlor, forget it!

Homework

Play both Baby Hardways and Daddy Hardways tonight, one game each. Compare your highs and lows, the same way I did with the two sample games in tables 6.1 and 6.2. Also compare the lengths of your longest and second-longest losing streaks.

Let your progressions run free. See how high they drift or don't drift. Let them run all the way up to $100 per bet if need be just to see what finally happens. See if they actually do drift back to zero again in the end. See for yourself what kind of profit they turn in, there on your kitchen table at least.

Be sure to correct properly. The progressions on the Hard 4 and Hard 10 (true 8 to 1, pays 7 to 1) both get corrected by $10 after every win, remember, while the progressions on the Hard 6 and Hard 8 (true 10 to 1, pays 9 to 1) get corrected by $12.

7

Any Craps

This is probably not the place to get into a discussion of karma, since you're simply looking for a book of gambling systems that work, but if it's true that there are casinos out there using rigged tables, even just a few of them, then the karmic implications are enormous. Could you imagine cheating the elderly out of their Social Security checks, what kind of entry that creates in the heavenly record books, not to mention luring emotionally troubled compulsive gamblers into ever-deeper anguish and misery with trick tables. Could you imagine destroying a compulsive gambler's life like that, watching him deteriorate as he comes back again and again, and you all the while deliberately cheating him just for the sake of the money you can take from him, knowing full well the whole time that somewhere back home probably an entire family is being destroyed by this person's emotional illness. Can you imagine someone making a living from such a thing? If ever there was such a thing as blood money, this would be it.

It is said that in Monte Carlo when a person commits suicide without any money in his pockets, the police immediately stuff some money in his pockets so people will think the victim killed himself because of world-weariness rather than gambling losses.

Does hell have a pit deep enough for such tricksters? How many suicides a year do Atlantic City and Las Vegas average?

The compulsive gamblers would certainly be the most pitiful victims of such a casino, but they would probably be a relative minority. Probably most of the people victimized by such a house would be ordinary naive citizens, people who would not know they'd been swindled until they heard about the scam years later. Even then it's likely some would not believe it was *them* but think it must apply to someone else.

The System Itself

Any Craps is mathematically the same as Baby Hardways (a true 8 to 1 paying 7 to 1), except that Any Craps is played on

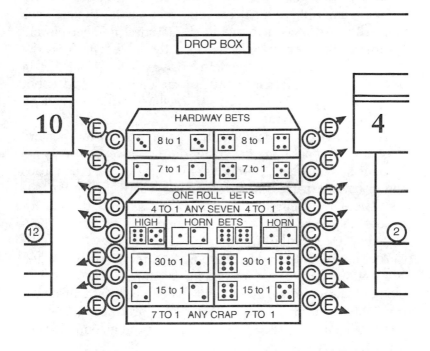

Fig. 7.1. The Center of the Craps Layout

the Any Craps wager. Have a look at fig. 7.1 please, the Center of the Craps Layout:

Off on both sides of the table are the Pass Line and the Don't Pass line, as we saw before, but in the center now we see a whole bunch of other bets available. If you look carefully you'll notice a whole string of encircled capital E's running up both sides of the center, and just to the inside of them a matching string of encircled capital C's. The E's stand for *eleven* and the C's stand for *craps*. Pay no attention to the rectangle at the bottom marked "7 TO 1 ANY CRAPS 7 TO 1". I don't know why that's there, the dealers never use it, they always use the C's in the circles instead. Likewise the encircled E's for eleven. No dealer ever puts the chips for an eleven bet in the eleven rectangle just above and to the right of the "7 TO 1 ANY CRAPS 7 TO 1" box; they'll always use the encircled E's instead.

You could write a small encyclopedia on the superstitions craps shooters have surrounding the mystical number eleven. It's one of the most popular bets on the table, which is why there are so many of those encircled E's on the layout, but in reality it's an unattractive bet. The true odds are 17 to 1, but the payoff is only 15 to 1, not 16 to 1, which means not enough payoff for such extreme risk.

The encircled C's, on the other hand, offer a much more reasonable proposition, an easier-on-the-nerves 8 to 1, no more risky than Baby Hardways. A bet on Any Craps means you're betting that the next roll of the dice will be a 2, 3, or 12. (These, you will recall, are the ones that cause the shooter to lose, or "crap out," if they appear on the first roll. That's why they're called the Craps.)

You open with $1 and increase by $1 after every loss. When you win, the formula for correction, as always, is the true odds plus two extra in order to create the all-important drift downward. Since the true odds in Any Craps are 8 to 1, the correction factor is 8 + 2 = $10 knocked off the amount of your bet after every win.

Mathematical Analysis

Let's take a look at an actual game of Any Craps. Have a look at table 7.1, please.

Table 7.1
Any Craps

Bet No.	Amount	Decision	Total Out	Total In	Profit
1	$1	L	$1		-$1
2	2	L	3		-3
3	3	L	6		-6
4	4	L	10		-10
5	5	L	15		-15
6	6	L	21		-21
7	7	L	28		-28
8	8	W	36	$64	28
9	1	W	37	72	35
10	1	L	38		34
11	2	L	40		32
12	3	L	43		29
13	4	W	47	104	57
14	1	L	48		56
15	2	L	50		54
16	3	L	53		51
17	4	L	57		47
18	5	L	62		42
19	6	L	68		36
20	7	L	75		29
21	8	L	83		21
22	9	L	92		12
23	10	L	102		2
24	11	L	113		-9
25	12	L	125		-21
26	13	L	138		-34
27	14	L	152		-48
28	15	L	167		-63
29	16	W	183	232	49
30	6	L	189		43
31	7	L	196		36
32	8	L	204		28
33	9	W	213	304	91

BET No.	AMOUNT	DECISION	TOTAL OUT	TOTAL IN	PROFIT
34	1	L	214		90
35	2	L	216		88
36	3	L	219		85
37	4	L	223		81
38	5	L	228		76
39	6	L	234		82
40	7	L	241		75
41	8	L	249		67
42	9	L	258		58
43	10	L	268		48
44	11	L	279		37
45	12	W	291	400	109
46	2	L	293		107
47	3	L	296		104
48	4	L	300		100
49	5	L	305		95
50	6	L	311		89
51	$7	W	$318	$456	$138
(52)	(1)				

Mathematically this should have been kissing cousin to the Baby Hardways game played in table 6.1, where the high was $174 and the low –$153. Both of them were true 8 to 1 paying 7 to 1. And yet we see that this game was unmistakably more moderate, wasn't it? Here the extremes weren't nearly as extreme, a high of only $138 (No. 51) and a low of only –$63 (No. 28).

Why? How can it be that identical odds produce such obviously different results? It's the Law of Probability. What it really says is not how it will be or should be but only what you'll *average* over the long run. If you average together enough Any Craps games you'll discover (at home at least) that your overall averages, as your data builds, move ever closer to a perfect 8 to 1. But as for predicting any given game, the truth is you never know.

A Frank Evaluation

Any Craps is a winner, one of the very best systems in this book. Since you're going to be playing it invisibly you'll be able to get down only one bet in your progression for each table you visit. We covered this before. You have to spend the day drifting through every table of every casino in town, playing simultaneous progressions on Any Craps, plus each of the Hardways, plus Pass/Don't Pass, plus all the other manageable bets besides, betting the next bet in each of your progressions each time you change tables—the craps progressions in the craps section, the roulette progressions in the roulette section, etc. To each boxperson it'll seem like one random bet on each of the more popular bets on his table by a person who comes and goes so quickly there isn't even time to get much of a fix on him. Given even a moderately busy day, they'll never spot you for a system player.

Homework

Any Craps moves along much, much faster than Baby or Daddy Hardways when you play them on your kitchen table because with Any Craps you get a fresh bet for each new roll of the dice. No gambling system could ever move faster than this. In a casino, on the other hand, they move at the same speed (for you at least) because you're only getting in one bet per progression per table.

In the last chapter you saw how profitable a true 8 to 1 (Baby Hardways) can be. Now the idea is not merely how profitable but also *how quickly* you can make all that money, at least there on your kitchen table.

Your homework is to play an hour's worth of very quick Any Craps progressions (and they *will* be quick, you'll see) just to see what kind of money you can rack up in an hour's time.

Once again, don't set limits in your test game. Since it's only for practice, run the progression all the way up to $100 or more if need be.

What will impress you this time, even more than the amount you make, is the *speed* with which you attain it. When you get done, pause and reflect that you made it all *in a single hour.*

8

Free Odds

Free Odds is by far the most elegant of all the systems in this book mathematically. It has an inner harmony and beauty which is a quantum shift upward from the kind of inner harmony and beauty found in the other systems, entitling it to a special place among the systems, most assuredly. If Einstein and Newton were alive today and reading this book, Free Odds would be the system they'd go for, no question about it. It may be the last word in what higher mathematics can do to a craps table.

The System Itself

Free Odds consists of playing two, three, or even four (your choice) simultaneous games of Half Peak, one on the Pass Line using $1 betting units, a normal game of Half Peak in other words, and the other(s) on the free odds, using $2, $5, or even $10 betting units. This is a deliberate and important imbalance.

Now of course you're already asking, "What are the free odds?" This will take some explaining.

I'm sure you remember the rules of craps, right? Each game begins with what's called the "come-out" roll. If the shooter rolls 7 or 11 on the come-out roll, he automatically wins; 2, 3, or 12 he automatically loses; and if he rolls any other number, that number becomes "the point." The object of the game from then on is to roll the point again before rolling a 7. If the shooter is lucky enough to roll the point again before rolling a 7, he wins. If the 7 comes first, he loses. You remember all this from chapter 4, of course.

The difficulty is that the 7 comes up more often than any other number. Take another look at the dice paradigm please, table 5.1. Out of 36 possible combinations, six of them amount to a 7. By contrast, only three of them amount to a 4. Therefore the likelihood of a 7 being rolled is exactly twice as great as the likelihood of a 4 being rolled.

So if the point is 4, the shooter is twice as likely to lose as he is to win. He's twice as likely to roll a 7 as he is to roll a 4. This amounts to a 2-to-1 bet and you can bet it if you like. It's called taking odds. Let's say you've bet $10 on the Pass Line. The shooter rolls the come-out roll and it's a 4. The point is now 4, and the object of the game for the shooter is to roll another 4 before rolling a 7. The odds against him are exactly 2 to 1. At this point you can just say to the dealer, "I'd like to take odds, please," and plunk down an additional bet, say $10, right next to your Pass Line bet but on the outside of the Pass Line, where it says NO CALL BETS in fig. 3.1, not inside the Pass Line where your other bet is. What this means is that you've placed a second bet. Now, in addition to your $10 bet on the Pass Line, which will pay 1 to 1 if it wins, you have a second bet down, this one a $10 bet that the 4 will be rolled before a 7.

Since the odds against you are 2 to 1, the payoff is 2 to 1. If the 4 does come in before the 7, you get back your $10 plus $20 from the house, and all this is *in addition to* your $10 bet on the Pass Line and the $10 the house pays you if the shooter wins.

Now what makes the free odds so thought-provoking, so thoroughly different from all the other bets in the casino, is that they really are free. There's no house edge. Remember when I first discussed Half Peak I said the house had a 1.42 percent edge on the Pass Line and I commented about what a good bet this was. Well, the *free* odds go this an infinite step better. On the free odds the house has *no edge at all.* It really is 50–50, you against them. The only hitch is that you must already have a bet down on the Pass Line to be able to play the free odds.

So consider this in your head, a second game of Half Peak played on the 2-to-1 free odds. First of all, this second game is intermittent. The 2-to-1 free odds are available only about one-sixth of the time, on average, because that's approximately how often there's a point of 4 or 10, and it's only when there's a point of 4 or 10 that the house offers you 2-to-1 free odds.

Also, the 2-to-1 game of Half Peak differs from the Pass Line game of Half Peak in that you reduce the bet by $2 after every win, not $1, because the bet and the payoff are both 2 to 1, not 1 to 1, as on the Pass Line.

Other than that, it's just an ordinary game of Half Peak like any other. You just follow the progression up and down the scale, and when you finally work your way back down to half your peak, you quit and start the progression all over again. (Since each of these Free Odds progressions is a separate game of Half Peak, they all reach half their peaks at different times. Therefore, the game of Free Odds has no mathematical conclusion: you just quit when you want to.)

As it is with the 2-to-1 free odds anytime the point is 4 or 10, so it is with the 3-to-2 free odds the house offers you any-time the point is 5 or 9, your *third* simultaneous game of Half Peak. Look again at table 5.1, please.

You see that out of thirty-six possible dice combinations, four of them amount to a 5, and four of them amount to a 9.

Thus, if the point is 5 or 9, the odds of rolling the point before rolling a 7 are exactly 6 to 4, or 3 to 2 (same thing), and again, you just plunk your chips down on the outside of the Pass Line and say, "I'd like to take odds, please." If you win, the dealer pays you $3 for every $2 in your bet.

Now please note carefully that while theory says you must reduce your bet on this third simultaneous game by $3 after every win and increase it by $2 after every loss, this is impossible under the house rules because for the house to pay you 3 to 2, your bet must always be for an *even* number of dollars. If you try to reduce your bet by $3 after a win, your next bet in the progression will then be for an *odd* number of dollars, a technical impossibility which the dealer will not allow. Therefore, in your third Half Peak game, the one you play anytime the point is 5 or 9, you have to decrease your bet by $6 after every win, not $3, and increase it by $4 after each loss, not $2, so your bets will always be for an even number of dollars, never an odd number.

The same is true for the 6-to-5 free odds the house offers you anytime the point is 6 or 8, your *fourth* simultaneous Half Peak game if you can hack it. Table 5.1 shows that the true likelihood of a 6 or 8 being rolled before a 7 is 6 to 5. Theory says you would decrease the bet by $6 after every loss, but for the house to pay you 6 to 5, your bet must always be for an amount that can be divided evenly by the number 5. Thus, in your fourth Half Peak game you must decrease the bet by $30 after every win and increase it by $25 after every loss. This amounts to a $5 betting unit, very high.

Now before we go any further, I have to explain to you that there's a limit to how much the house will let you bet on a free odds bet. Usually that limit is equal to two times the amount you've got riding on the Pass Line, what's called Double Odds, but I've seen houses that offered at much as *Quintuple* Odds, five times the amount.

Mathematical Analysis

The illustration game of Free Odds played in table 8.1 would have required a minimum of Triple Odds because the $120 odds taken in bet No. 2 would have been illegal otherwise.

The very first thing we notice about our hypothetical game in table 8.1 is the action on the Pass Line. The opening bet is $47, absurdly high. That's because the more you have riding on the Pass Line the more you can bet on the free odds, which in turn gives you that much more flexibility with your free-odds progressions. This is part of what makes Free Odds so complicated to play in the real world. No cautious person is going to open a Half Peak game at $47. You could run into poor luck. Even if you place only one bet per table and conceal from the house completely the fact that you're using a killer system on them, you could still run into ill fortune.

Table 8.1
Free Odds

(N = natural, C = craps)

Bet No.	Amount and Decision	Amount of Free Odds Bet 4 or 10 @2:1	5 or 9 @3:2	6 or 8 @6:5	Bet Total In	Overall Total Out	Overall Total In	Overall Profit
1	$47W	N	N	N	$94	$47	$94	$47
2	46W			$120	356	213	450	237
3	45W	N	N	N	90	258	540	235
4	44 L		$60			362		178
5	45W	N	N	N	90	407	630	223
6	44 L		64			515		115
7	45W			90	198	650	828	178
8	44 L	30				724		104
9	45W	N	N	N	90	769	918	149
10	44W			60	220	873	1,138	265
11	43W			30	152	946	1,290	344
12	42W	N	N	N	84	988	1,374	386
13	41 L			0		1,029		345
14	42 L	C	C	C		1,071		303

Bet No.	Amount and Decision	Free Odds 4 or 10 @2:1	Free Odds 5 or 9 @3:2	Amount of Bet 6 or 8 @6:5	Bet Total In	Overall Total Out	Overall Total In	Overall Profit
15	43 L		68			1,182		192
16	44 L		25		1,251		123	
17	45 L		72			1,368		6
18	46 L	31				1,445		−71
19	47W		76		284	1,568	1,658	90
20	46W	N	N	N	92	1,614	1,750	136
21	45W		70		265	1,729	2,015	286
22	44W			50	198	1,823	2,213	390
23	43 L		64			1,930		283
24	44 L	32				2,006		207
25	45 L			20		2,071		142
26	46W			45	191	2,162	2,404	242
27	45W	33			189	2,240	2,593	353
28	44 L	C	C	C		2,284		309
29	45 L			15		2,344		249
30	46 L		68			2,458		135
31	47W	N	N	N	94	2,505	2,687	182
32	46W			40	180	2,591	2,867	276
33	45 L		72			2,708		159
34	46 L			10		2,764		103
35	47 L			35		2,846		21
36	48 L	C	C	C		2,894		−27
37	49 L	31				2,974		−107
38	50W	32			196	3,056	3,063	7
39	49 L	C	C	C		3,105		−42
40	50 L	30				3,185		−122
41	51W	N	N	N	102	3,236	3,165	−71
42	50W	N	N	N	100	3,286	3,265	−21
43	49 L	31				3,366		−101
44	50W			60	232	3,476	3,497	21
45	49 L			30		3,555		−58
46	50W		76		290	3,681	3,787	106
47	49W			55	219	3,785	4,006	221
48	48 L	32				3,865		141
49	49 L	C	C	C		3,914		92
50	50W	N	N	N	100	3,964	4,106	142
51	49W	N	N	N	98	4,013	4,204	191
52	48W	N	N	N	96	4,061	4,300	239
53	47 L		70			4,178		122
54	48W			$25	151	4,251	4,451	200
55	$47W		$64		$286	$4,362	$4,737	$375

(56)

The first bet is recorded as a "natural." That's what the N's stand for in table 8.1, which means the bet was a winner on the come-out roll by reason of either a 7 or an 11. No free odds on this one.

On the second bet the point was 6 and the odds $120 at 6 to 5. This is an much larger amount of money than usual but the 6-to-5 progression requires $5 betting units, remember.

A win turned the $120 into $120 + $144 = $264. From then on table 8.1 tells the story: a high of $390 on bet No. 22, a low of -$122 on bet No. 40, and a conclusion at bet No. 55, $375 ahead.

Let's take a look at the different elements of this Free Odds game, the four separate progressions of which it's composed. The primary progression, of course, is the one on the Pass Line. This began at $47 but ran all the way down to $41 on the thirteenth bet, a nice early winning streak which was $386 ahead by bet No. 12. Then the luck drifted in the opposite direction, and by bet No. 41 the Pass Line bet was back up to $51, $4 higher than at the beginning. This was the game low which I just mentioned, and then by bet No. 55, the last, the Overall Profit column recovered to the point of being $375 ahead. At the end the Pass Line bet was back at $47, the starting point, generally a good sign of a profitable time to quit.

But the game high of $390 ahead came on bet No. 22, when the Pass Line bet was $44, sort of in the middle of nowhere. Why is that? Because from bet No. 19 to bet No. 22, a space of only four bets, we were able to get in three different free odds bets—for $76, $70, and $50—and all three of them won. Thus, we hit the game high at a time when the Pass Line progression had lost six of the previous ten bets, but it didn't matter because the Pass Line progression with its $1 betting units was small potatoes. The real action was in the free odds progressions, and when *they* came in, especially the $76 and $70 both at 3 to 2, that's when we hit the game high.

The same applies to bet No. 18 where we were -$71 in the hole in spite of the Pass Line bet being $46, $1 *less* than where we started. And the reason again is that the Pass Line progression was small potatoes compared with what was happening with the free odds progressions, which in this case incurred three nasty losses. How amazing that we could move from -$71 in the hole to the game high of $390 in the space of just four progressive steps. Yet we did, and the reason was that the free-odds progressions, while intermittent, proved overwhelming.

A Frank Evaluation

Utterly impractical for all of its mathematical elegance. I think by now you can see what makes Free Odds such an fascinating game. You're playing four separate progressions simultaneously (albeit intermittently), but on only one of the four progressions does the house have an edge. On the other three it has no edge at all. You and the house are on an even footing. Moreover, on the one progression where the house does have an edge, you're betting only $1 betting units and cutting your risk to an absolute minimum, while on the other three progressions, where you have no disadvantage, you're betting much larger betting units and boosting your profitability to a maximum.

The great disadvantage is that you have to place much heavier bets than usual on the Pass Line in order to be able to utilize the free odds adequately, and this in turn means phenomenal risk in case you run into a bad losing streak, not to mention the possibility that you may unwittingly wander into one of those rigged casinos we've been hypothesizing about, in which case you'd blow your invisibility immediately by betting such a pattern, wouldn't you?

Homework

Try a Free Odds game. It's fine craps practice and once you learn it all the other craps systems will pale by comparison.

9

Tailspin

Even if there should be a rigged casino somewhere—and it
hasn't happened yet, please note—the sad truth as we all know
is that corruption and dishonesty are to be found in many
other places in this world of ours, not just some casino.
Indeed, it all too often seems that corruption and dishonesty
are on the rise in our society. Is it a myth that things were
more honest and honorable back in the Eisenhower era before
the anti-establishmentarianism of the 1960's (what Newt Gin-
grich calls counterculture, although the real counterculture—
flower power and the hippies—was never political), or was the
duplicity just better concealed? Did the 1960's and the cultur-
al revolution it spawned bring more duplicity and less integrity, or did it merely turn a spotlight on that which was former-
ly hidden from view? In other words, is the modern world less
moral or is immorality merely getting more attention now?

What do you think? If over the course of your life you've
become less moral, you'll probably imagine that society has
declined too. If, on the other hand, the years have matured
you and made you more moral, you'll likely imagine society's
getting better too. If you've stayed the same, you'll likely imagine the world too has stayed the same.

The English language contains two fascinating words, integrity and duplicity. They're opposites, but a lot of people seemingly don't realize it. If we're to judge from the way human lives are lived, there are evidently people out there who don't realize they have the option of going through life with one face instead of two. Integrity is the state of being whole, of being one and not being two. It's being real and not phony, having one face instead of two. How many people do you know who are real and not phony? How many do you know who are phony and not real?

Actually there's almost nobody who's 100 percent phony or 100 percent real. We're all a mix. This real/phony thing is actually a continuum, a spectrum, and the real question is not are you real or phony, but where in the middle do you fit in? Are you dead center or are you toward the real end? Or are you toward the phony end? (Actually, real and phony are only one pair of many such continua: there's also positive/negative, mature/immature, brave/cowardly, cool/repressed, to name just a few.)

When we think of the word *corruption* we normally think of a material corruption of some kind, but there's also such a thing as corruption of spirit. Human souls evolve over the course of a lifetime, or at least they have the potential to. We all know that human character comes in different sizes. We know, for example, what's meant when we speak of someone as being a "small" person. It has nothing to do with height or weight.

The point is, we all have the potential to become either larger or smaller people as time goes by. We actually do have freedom of choice in this and we have to pay full price for any mistakes. Our spiritual evolution then depends to a considerable extent on this choice we're presented with every time we get the opportunity to decide whether to be real or phony, whether to have one face or two. Choosing integrity makes you a tiny bit larger each time. Choosing duplicity makes you a tiny bit smaller.

Therefore the advantage of choosing integrity instead of duplicity is that your character evolves slowly for the better over time, rather than for the worse. Better yet, your children inherit this largeness of character and spirit without your ever having to teach it to them. They learn it just from watching you.

In practical terms what it comes down to is, this world is just a giant campground for the development of human souls. Develop them right and they grow larger. Do it wrong and they end up smaller.

The System Itself

Tailspin is a very, very simple system, perhaps the ultimate in simplicity. You'll quickly see it's also very, very risky, sort of like Russian Roulette played with a revolver that has dozens of chambers and only one bullet. The likelihood of disaster is fairly small but the possibility is there. It's played on the Any Craps bet, the one where you win if a 2, 3 or 12 is rolled on the next roll. It pays 7 to 1 against a true 8 to 1, one of the more reasonable propositions on the craps table, a fair payoff with comparatively modest risk.

Tailspin starts out just like the Any Craps system in chapter 3, but as soon as you reach a bet of $8 you don't bet $8, you bet $9 instead. This is because as soon as you get past $7 you start increasing your bet by $2, not $1; but only until you reach $14 or more (or 2 times 7, since it's a 7-to-1 payoff), at which point you begin increasing by $3 after every loss. But again, as soon as you reach $3 × $7 = $21, you start increasing by $4 after every loss.

Past $28 you increase by $5 after every loss. Past $35 you increase by $6 after every loss. Past $42 you increase by $7, etc., all the way up to the house limit, until you finally get a craps, that is, until someone finally rolls a 2, 3 or 12. At that point the game ends. That's what makes it so simple: *it takes only one win*. As soon as somebody finally rolls a craps, however long it takes, however much money you've invested in your progression, the instant that craps appears you've won back everything you've invested, plus a nice profit besides.

In the normal course of things you should get one craps for every nine throws of the dice. Superficially, then, the system seems foolproof. What's the problem?

Mathematical Analysis

The problem is the speed at which your progression accelerates if by some mischance you don't happen to get a craps. Take a look at table 9.1, please. Pay special attention to the second column, the one labeled "Amount." It starts to move up pretty fast, doesn't it? At bet No. 20 you're putting up only $60, but take a look at bet No. 40. Now you're talking $911. That's quite a difference. Your progression has accelerated like a rocket sled.

Table 9.1
Tailspin

BET No.	AMOUNT	TOTAL OUT	WINNING PAYOFF, WHEN AND IF	PROFIT WHEN AND IF
1	$1	$1	$8	$7
2	2	3	16	13
3	3	6	24	18
4	4	10	32	22
5	5	15	40	25
6	6	21	48	27
7	7	28	56	28
8	9	37	72	35
9	11	48	88	40
10	13	61	104	43
11	15	76	140	44
12	18	94	144	50
13	21	115	168	53
14	25	140	200	60
15	29	169	232	63
16	34	203	272	69

Bet No.	Amount	Total Out	Winning Payoff, WHEN AND IF	Profit WHEN AND IF
17	39	242	312	70
18	45	287	360	73
19	52	339	416	77
20	60	399	480	81
21	69	468	552	84
22	79	547	632	85
23	91	638	728	90
24	104	742	832	90
25	119	861	952	91
26	137	998	1,096	98
27	157	1,155	1,256	101
28	180	1,335	1,440	105
29	206	1,541	1,648	107
30	236	1,777	1,888	111
31	271	2,048	2,168	120
32	310	2,358	2,480	122
33	355	2,713	2,840	127
34	406	3,119	3,248	129
35	465	3,584	3,720	136
36	532	4,116	4,256	140
37	609	4,725	4,872	147
38	697	5,422	5,576	154
39	797	6,219	6,376	157
40	$911	$7,130	$7,288	$158

If you think that's bad, take a look at the third column, the one labeled "Total Out." That heading starts to have a double meaning after a while. On bet No. 20, where the amount of your bet is up to $60, the total amount you've laid out is $399, a pretty substantial amount of money. But take a look now at bet No. 40. Here you're betting $911, but your total amount laid out is now an incredible $7,130! I have friends who don't make that much money in a whole year, yet that's how much you'll be called upon to put up if you start this game and happen to go 40 rolls of the dice without a 2, 3, or 12 appearing.

And yet it's profitable. Check out the last column, the one labeled "Profit." Assuming you did run into ghastly, hideous luck and had to sweat out a run of forty losses before a craps finally came in, you'd still have all your money back plus $158 besides. How utterly amazing, if you've got the nerve to try it.

The secret is that you keep increasing the rate of increase as you get deeper and deeper in, a profoundly scary thing to do, but it works. It's a little like the idea of correcting a tailspin in an airplane by pushing the stick *forward* instead of pulling it backward. (That's where the name of the system comes from.) It seems on the face of it like the worst possible thing to do, and yet if you do it, you come out fine—as long as a craps comes in.

But what if a craps doesn't come in?

Obviously the operative question here is how long can it go without any craps coming in? The answer is: a woefully long time, long enough to burn away every last one of your sins, and then some.

A Frank Evaluation

Risky. Really, really risky. I can admit with manageable shame that I myself have never had the guts actually to try this one in a casino for reasons which will be all too clear to you once you've finished this chapter's homework assignment.

Homework

Take the dice from your Monopoly game and see how many times you can roll them on the kitchen table without a 2, 3, or 12 appearing. One time I rolled them *187 times in a row* without a single craps appearing. I haven't even tried to calculate how much that hundred and eighty-seventh bet would have to be. The amount is surely above the house limit in any casino in the world. Actually, you'd be above the house limit in most casinos by the fiftieth roll, never mind the hundred and eighty-seventh.

As the layout says, any craps, as long as one finally does come in. But if one doesn't, brother, it means you didn't get your tailspin corrected after all. It means you hit the ground.

If you decide to play Tailspin to the house limit, always

round upward when calculating the next bet. If it comes out to an even amount with no fraction then bet a dollar more. That's what I did in table 9.1. Those are the first forty amounts you'll be betting. You may not survive. You may run out of paper on which to write all the IOUs. You'll see. This is why I have such deep reservations about Tailspin. Once you've gone 187 rolls without a single craps appearing, it'll all be much clearer to you.

The Tailspin approach may also work on the U.S. economy, interestingly enough. Everyone agrees Uncle Sam has lost some kind of economic vigor since Vietnam, but nobody seems to know what to do about it. The Tailspin approach would be simply to jumpstart the economy with borrowed money again, the same way President Reagan did. We tried all this with Trickle Down, but this time we're going to make it Trickle Up. The idea is to divide the windfall evenly among *all* Americans, not just the rich, but with two careful rules: (1) they can spend no more than half of it; they have to save at least half, and (2) they have to keep it in a *local* bank, they can't go put it in the stock market or some fund that's just going to turn around and put it in the stock market. The idea is to use it to capitalize the local situation, whatever it is, and trust that the local wisdom will be able to manage the rest.

The idea is to have the money fill the country like rain saturating a lawn, not like a creek trickling through a desert. That would do it, that would correct the Tailspin, but who's got guts enough to try?

Legend says the first pilot ever to have guts enough to try it in an airplane was a woman, Amelia Earhart. She had guts enough to try, a woman. Men, take note.

Roulette Systems

10

Two-Step

Craps is a fun game, in my opinion the most fun of any of the games in the casino, but for the beginner the pace can really be bewildering sometimes, which may help explain the enduring popularity of roulette, the classic European casino game and an appealingly simple concept, certainly when compared with craps.

Roulette is a European game. Craps is American. That may go a long way toward explaining why it is that the two of them are so different in character. In craps players holler and roar and frequently explode into bursts of yelling so loud that people stop and turn their heads all over the casino. It's the last word in casualness and informality, which is typically the American way of doing things. Roulette, by comparison, comes across as almost stuffy.

Actually, if anything, we Americans have greatly *informalized* the game of roulette compared with the way the Europeans get into it with their black ties and tuxedos, but by American standards roulette is still a very formal game. It's still the part of the casino where the fashionable ladies go to be seen in their diamonds and chinchilla, and in the broadest sense of the word the roulette people, the players, dealers, and of course the boxpeople really do their very best to keep together a class act. Everyone speaks in a soft voice, even the winners, and the pace is very dignified. Purists make it a point never to look or sound as if they're enjoying themselves but rather to act as if they couldn't care less, no matter what happens.

This is as alien from an American point of view as everything else in Europe, but again, in an American casino you don't have to get involved in these social games if you don't want to. You can just walk right up to the table and plunk your money down without so much as a *bon soir*, if you prefer, and I recommend it. That and a good crowded table.

The first thing you notice when changing from craps to roulette is that roulette players sit, they don't stand. If you've got hemorrhoids or sore feet, roulette's the better game for you. It's a beautifully simple game: the tourneur spins the wheel in one direction, shoots the little ball in the opposite direction, and everybody waits to see where it lands.

There are thirty-seven different possibilities in single-zero roulette and thirty-eight in double-zero. The numbers run from zero to thirty-six inclusive and you can bet on any of all of them as you please. Are roulette wheels rigable also? In earlier decades John Scarne exposed a magnet gaff in the table under the wheel, not in the wheel itself, the earlier mode of chicanery. Today's suspicious approach would be the same as the one for craps, to recognize that (1) there are numerous possibilities for running profitable progressions on a roulette layout, but that (2) you'll have to pick a busy time *and* adequately conceal from the house what you're doing. The method is to spend the whole day drifting slowly from wheel to wheel, same as with the craps tables, betting the next bet in each of your progressions every time you sit down to a new wheel but never betting two bets in the same progression at the same wheel, in order to make sure the house never sees any progressive betting. All you want the house to see is apparently random bets. Only you know that they're all parts of intermittent progressions, all being played simultaneously.

Once again, with roulette as with craps, we're confronted with this mystery of why the systems work so nicely at home but not nearly so well in the casinos. You will just have to be patient with this part.

The payoff on a single-number bet is 35 to 1, which means that for every unit in your bet you get back thirty-five units from the house, plus your bet, equal to thirty-six times the amount of your bet. This is a spectacular payoff, but the problem is it comes only once in every thirty-eight turns. Even without that remote possibility of a rigged wheel, it poses a problem.

Going for the 35-to-1 long shot is the most exotic way to play roulette, single- or double-zero, and there's a specific gambling system designed to accommodate the 35-to-1 shot. It's called Lucky Number (see chapter 17), and it's the riskiest of all the systems in this book, one of a group I call the holistics.

The beginning system for roulette is called Two-Step and it corresponds in many ways to Half Peak. Look at fig. 10.1, please. For both the single-zero and the double-zero roulette

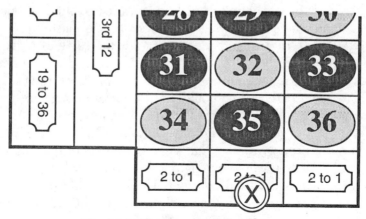

Fig. 10.1. The "2 to 1" Column Bets

tables the thirty-six numbers are laid out in three even columns with the zero(s) laid out across the top, near the wheel. At the bottom of each column is the space where you put your chips if you want to bet that column. It's marked "2 to 1" (letter X). This means, of course, that columns are a 2-to-1 bet. Pass and Don't Pass were 1-to-1 bets, which meant if you bet $3 and won you got back $3 from the house in addition to your $3. But on a 2-to-1 bet, if you bet $3 and win you get back $6 from the house in addition to your $3. We ran into something like this not long ago in chapter 8, "Free Odds": the free odds on points of either four or ten were also 2 to 1, the same payoff as the columns in roulette except that with the free odds it really is a true 2-to-1 bet, whereas with the columns in roulette you have the zeros to contend with. They lengthen the true odds to slightly longer than 2 to 1, but not so much more as to make it unprofitable. Even with a double-zero wheel you're still talking about a house edge of only one in nineteen turns, which is to say, only a shade over 5 percent.

Since each column is a 2-to-1 bet with a 2-to-1 payoff, you reduce the bet on a column by *two* units after every win, although you still raise it by only one unit after every loss. (There's no correction factor here for drift. The correction comes at half peak.) It's the same once again as it is in Free Odds on points of four or ten, the second of your four Half Peak games if you're playing Free Odds to the maximum.

Other than that, a game of Two-Step is the same as a game of Half Peak. You want to start at least $12 (or twelve units) above the house minimum in order to be able to store at least half a dozen early wins, should you be lucky enough to have that many come your way. In a typical casino this means an opening bet of $15 at least, maybe more like $17, making Two-Step more expensive than Half Peak but also more profitable. In Half Peak you were winning one-half unit per bet. In Two-Step you win one full unit per bet. The hitch, unfortunately, is that the pace at craps is almost always faster than at roulette, but not so much faster that Two-Step isn't competitive.

If you begin with an opening bet of $15, the Half Peak concept doesn't even come into play until your progression reaches $35. At $35 Half Peak becomes $17.50, or $18 since you can't bet fractions of dollars, and then, assuming you work your way back down to $18 before reaching a higher peak, you quit at $18 and begin afresh at $15 instead of betting $16 after winning at $18.

Mathematical Analysis

Table 10.1
Two-Step

Bet No.	Amount	Decision	Total Out	Total In	Profit
1	$15	L	$15		−$15
2	16	L	31		−31
3	17	L	48		−48
4	18	W	66	$54	−12
5	16	W	82	102	20
6	14	W	96	144	48
7	12	W	108	180	72
8	10	W	118	210	92
9	8	L	126		84
10	9	L	135		75
11	10	L	145		65
12	11	L	156		54
13	12	L	168		42
14	13	W	181	249	68
15	11	L	192		57
16	12	W	204	285	81
17	10	L	214		71
18	11	L	225		60
19	12	L	237		48
20	13	W	250	324	74
21	11	L	261		63
22	12	W	273	360	87
23	10	L	283		77
24	11	W	294	393	99
25	9	W	303	420	117
26	7	L	310		110
27	8	W	318	444	126

BET NO.	AMOUNT	DECISION	TOTAL OUT	TOTAL IN	PROFIT
28	6	W	324	462	138
29	4	L	328		134
30	5	L	333		129
31	6	L	339		123
32	7	L	346		116
33	8	L	354		108
34	9	L	363		99
35	10	L	373		89
36	11	L	384		78
37	12	L	396		66
38	13	L	409		53
39	14	L	423		39
40	15	L	438		24
41	16	L	454		8
42	17	L	471		−9
43	18	L	489		−27
44	19	W	508	519	11
45	17	L	525		−6
46	18	W	543	573	30
47	16	L	559		14
48	17	W	576	624	48
49	15	L	591		33
50	16	L	607		17
51	17	L	624		0
52	18	L	642		−18
53	19	W	661	681	20
54	17	W	678	732	54
55	15	W	693	777	84
56 (57)	$13	W	$706	$816	$110

The demonstration game in table 10.1 seems statistically irregular, but in the real world virtually all games are irregular. Even though the columns are a 2-to-1 bet, I won five of the first eight bets, and by the end of the eighth bet I was already $92 ahead. Such luck rarely lasts, of course, and by the thirteenth bet my $92 was already back down to $42. From there on the wins and losses were more typically distributed until the twenty-fourth bet, when I got another short lucky streak and won four of the next five. That was when the profit peaked at $138, the game high at bet No. 28.

Notice that on bet No. 29 I was betting only $4, a mere $1 above the minimum at a $3 wheel, which thoroughly vindicates the strategy of opening with a high enough bet to be able to store at least six early wins, should you be lucky enough to get them.

Bet No. 28 may have brought my profit to a game high of $138, but immediately afterward I got hit with a brutal losing streak, losing fifteen in a row from bet No. 29 to bet No. 43. At that point, not only was the $138 profit gone, but I was even $27 in the hole. Luck came back, however. From bet No. 44 to bet No. 56 I enjoyed seven wins out of thirteen bets, and once again I quit while I was ahead on the sacred belief that any game where you quit while you're ahead is always a winning game.

This might be the time to point out that it's no coincidence at bet No. 54 that I had won precisely $54 in fifty-four bets at that point. The reason is because after bet $54 the amount of my bet had worked its way back to precisely $15 again, exactly the same amount I opened with. Remember now it's in the nature of the Two-Step system that it produces exactly one dollar profit per bet (or one unit profit per bet) if your luck works out to be exactly average. After bet No. 54, in which I bet $17 and won, my luck became exactly average again.

In fact, if you look back carefully at table 10.1, you'll see there were two other times in the game at which the bet had worked its way back to the same amount I opened with. At bet No. 40 and No. 49 I wagered precisely $15, and if you check you'll see that in both cases my profit prior to betting the $15 was exactly equal to $1 for each turn of the wheel. At the end of bet No. 39 I was $39 ahead and at the end of bet No. 48 I was $48 ahead.

A Frank Evaluation

All this would seem to make Two-Step an ideal roulette system for beginners, and it is. Glorious. But there's something much deeper here: there are only three columns. How invitingly limited. Is it possible to play all of them at once? That is, play three different games of Two-Step simultaneously at the same roulette wheel? And if so, what happens?

What happens is Trilogy, the system we're going to look at next, and a whole new way of looking at a roulette wheel.

Homework

Study the roulette layout at the beginning of this book. The time has come to familiarize yourself with it. Obtain a gaming guide from the casino, along with information about opening an account. If they ask you how much you're interested in wagering, tell them you don't know, it depends on current bond prices. An account can be a handy thing to have; you just deposit your chips and draw credit as needed. It saves you having to stand on line at the cashier's window and greatly warms the relationship between you and the house. If you're trying to stay invisible, though, opening an account may not always be helpful.

Play Two-Step. Get a toy roulette wheel, or write the numbers 1–36 plus 0 and 00 on 38 identical wood or plastic chips. Scrabble tiles or poker chips are just fine. Stick some masking tape on the back of each one and write the number on it. Then drop them all into a grab bag.

The purpose of this exercise is to accustom you to the idea of correcting by $2 after every win, instead of $1 as in Half Peak. This is a necessary preparation for Trilogy, the next system, and all the holistic systems to follow.

11

Trilogy

We all know that we have a physical environment, and by pouring pollutants into it we have to live in a polluted environment. But it's just as true that we have a spiritual environment, and if we pour pollutants into that, we have to live in a polluted spiritual environment.

All this ties together with souls and the evolution of their size over a lifetime because it's more than just individuals who vary in largeness and smallness over the course of time, it's whole societies as well—what we call societies, but what actually are spiritual environments.

The authors of the Talmud, who lived at the time of the Roman Empire, said of the spiritual level of the Jews who received the Torah at Mount Sinai more than a millennium earlier, "If we are as men, then they were as angels. And if they were as men, then we are as donkeys." This makes the point: societies too evolve spiritually. Choices between real or phony, brave or cowardly, positive or negative, etc., may take place on the individual level, but they affect the society around us as well. They add to the spiritual environment, and to whatever extent they add to it they help shape it.

The corruption of the individual assists the corruption of society in general, that much is plain enough. But what about the flip side, the healing? To what extent can a society be healed by the individuals in that society healing themselves? And just how far can that healing go?

And of course in the end to relate it to America, not to start waving a flag or anything like that, but merely to ask what's happening with the drift of American society? Are we as a nation getting larger or smaller? Will the Americans of the future see us as being on a spiritual level they themselves are no longer able to reach, or will they be on a far higher level than us as a result of our having cleaned up the pollution of the spiritual environment? Or will everything continue along pretty much as it always has been, some of us angels and some of us donkeys? Your answer, once again, is probably just a projection of your personal spiritual situation. As for the actual destiny of America, God decides that, just as He decides if you're going to make any money using these systems or not.

But can we by our moral choices influence His decisions? If He sees we're trying our best, does that move Him to help? Does He test us? How does a win or loss affect our future tests and opportunities?

The System Itself

Two-Step is a worthy system, all the more beautiful for its ease and simplicity, and to add to its charm it can also be played on the dozens instead of the columns. These are laid out along the edge of the inside, in between the inside and the even money bets. (See fig. 11.1, the Dozens.) They come in three varieties, 1–12, 13–24 and 25–36, and they're the same thing mathematically as the columns. What this means is that, if you're smart enough to stay invisible, Two-Step provides fully *six* new progressions for you to keep track of in that secret little notebook. Remember, you're playing many, many progressions at once, betting a single bet at every new roulette table

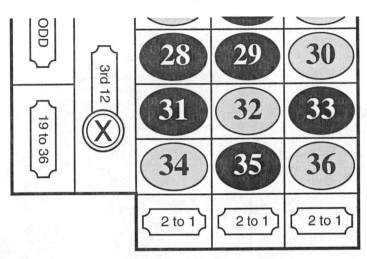

Fig. 11.1. The Dozens

you sit down to. In each case, the boxperson won't see anything except random bets all over the layout.

Mathematical Analysis

Trilogy is three separate games of Two-Step played at the same wheel. It's profitable because Two-Step is profitable and Trilogy is three separate games of Two-Step going on simultaneously.

Table 11.1 is a demonstration Trilogy game and clearly indicates what a hectic ride it can be. The very first thing you'll notice is that almost the entire game is spent in deficit, more than an hour of running at an unrelieved loss, until finally the cumulative weight of all those theoretical winnings begins to assert itself and force a profit. The play on this game was hectic due to above-average activity in the middle column. That column kept winning more than it should have, at the expense of the third column, which wasn't winning at all, or hardly at all. The first column, though, was just about average in wins and losses.

Let's consider table 11.1, column by column, as three separate games of Two-Step running side by side and see how they affect each other.

Table 11.1
Trilogy

AMOUNTS AND DECISIONS
(W = WIN)

BET No.	COL 1	D	COL 2	D	COL 3	D	TOTAL OUT	TOTAL IN	PROFIT
1	$18		$18	W	$18		$54	$54	$0
2	19	W	16		19		108	111	3
3	17	W	17		20		162	162	0
4	15		18	W	21		216	216	0
5	16		16	W	22		270	264	−6
6	17	W	14		23		324	315	−9
7	15		15	W	24		378	360	−18
8	16	W	13		25		432	408	−24
9	14		14	W	26		486	450	−36
10	15		12	W	27		540	486	−54
11	16		10		28	W	594	570	−24
12	17	W	11		26		648	621	−27
13	15		12		27	W	702	702	0
14	16		13	W	25		756	741	−15
15	17		11		26	W	810	819	9
16	18		12	W	24		864	855	−9
17	19		10	W	25		918	885	−33
18	20		8		26	W	972	963	−9
19	21	W	9		24		1,026	1,026	0
20	19		10		25	W	1,080	1,101	21
21	20		11		23	W	1,134	1,170	36
22	21		12	W	21		1,188	1,206	18
23	22		10	W	22		1,242	1,236	−6
24	23		8	W	23		1,296	1,260	−36
25	24		6	W	24		1,350	1,278	−72
26	25		4		25	W	1,404	1,296	−108
27	26	W	5		23		1,458	1,374	−84
28	24		6	W	24		1,512	1,392	−120
29	25		4		25	W	1,566	1,467	−99
30	26		5		23	W	1,620	1,536	−84
31	27		6		21	W	1,674	1,599	−75
32	28	W	7		19		1,728	1,683	−45
33	26		8	W	20		1,782	1,707	−75
34	27		6		21	W	1,836	1,770	−66
35	28	W	7		19		1,890	1,854	−36
36	26		8		20	W	1,944	1,914	−30
37	27		9	W	18		1,998	1,941	−57
38	28		7	W	19		2,052	1,962	−90

AMOUNTS AND DECISIONS
(W = WIN)

BET NO.	COL 1	D	COL 2	D	COL 3	D	TOTAL OUT	TOTAL IN	PROFIT
39	29		5		20	W	2,106	2,022	−84
40	30	W	6		18		2,160	2,112	−48
41	28	0	7	0	19	0	2,214	2,112	−102
42	29	W	8		20		2,271	2,199	−72
43	27	W	9		21		2,328	2,280	−48
44	25	W	10		22		2,385	2,355	−30
45	23		11	W	23		2,442	2,388	−54
46	24	W	9		24		2,499	2,460	−39
47	22	W	10		25		2,556	2,526	−30
48	20	W	11		26		2,613	2,586	−27
49	18		12	W	27		2,670	2,622	−48
50	19		10	W	28		2,727	2,652	−75
51	20		8	W	29		2,784	2,676	−108
52	21	W	6		30		2,841	2,739	−102
53	19		7		31	W	2,898	2,832	−66
54	20	0	8	0	29	0	2,955	2,832	−123
55	21		9	W	30		3,015	2,859	−156
56	22		7	W	31		3,075	2,880	−195
57	23	W	5		32		3,135	2,949	−186
58	21	W	6		33		3,195	3,012	−183
59	19		7	W	34		3,255	3,033	−222
60	20		5		35	W	3,315	3,138	−177
61	21		6	W	33		3,375	3,156	−219
62	22	W	4		34		3,435	3,222	−213
63	20		5		35	W	3,495	3,327	−168
64	21		6	W	33		3,555	3,345	−210
65	22	W	4		34		3,615	3,411	−204
66	20		5		35	W	3,675	3,516	−159
67	21		6		33	W	3,735	3,615	−120
68	22	W	7		31		3,795	3,681	−114
69	20	W	8		32		3,855	3,741	−114
70	18		9		33	W	3,915	3,840	−75
71	19		10		31	W	3,975	3,933	−42
72	20		11		29	W	4,035	4,020	−15
73	21		12	W	27		4,095	4,056	−39
74	22		10	W	28		4,155	4,086	−69
75	23	W	8		29		4,215	4,155	−60
76	21		9		30	W	4,275	4,245	−30
77	22		10	W	28		4,335	4,275	−60
78	23		8		29	W	4,395	4,362	−33
79	24		9	W	27		4,455	4,389	−66
80	25	W	7		28		4,515	4,464	−51

AMOUNTS AND DECISIONS
(W = WIN)

BET No.	COL 1	D	COL 2	D	COL 3	D	TOTAL OUT	TOTAL IN	PROFIT
81	23	W	8		29		4,575	4,533	−42
82	21		9	W	30		4,635	4,560	−75
83	22		7		31	W	4,695	4,653	−42
84	23		8		29	W	4,755	4,740	−15
85	24		9		27	W	4,815	4,821	6
86	25	W	10		25		4,875	4,896	21
87	23		11		26	W	4,935	4,974	39
88	24		12	W	24		4,995	5,010	15
89	25	W	10		25		5,055	5,085	30
90	23		11	W	26		5,115	5,118	3
91	24		9		27	W	5,175	5,199	24
92	25		10		25	W	5,235	5,274	39
93	26		11		23	W	5,295	5,343	48
94	27		12		21	W	5,355	5,406	51
95	28		13	W	19		5,415	5,445	30
96	29	0	11	0	20	0	5,475	5,445	−30
97	30	W	12		21		5,538	5,535	−3
98	28		13		22	W	5,601	5,601	0
99	29	W	14		20		5,664	5,688	24
100	27	W	15		21		5,727	5,769	42
101	25	W	16		22		5,790	5,844	54
102	23	W	17		23		5,853	5,913	60
103	21		18		24	W	5,916	5,985	69
104	22		19		22	W	5,979	6,051	72
105 (106)	$23	W	$20		$20		$6,042	$6,120	$78

Our first column was typical, starting at $18, reaching a low of $14 on the ninth turn, a high of $30 on the fortieth turn, and finishing reasonably at $21 on the one hundred and sixth turn.

The second column, too, began at $18, but plummeted. It won on the very first turn of the wheel and the amount of its bet immediately began falling and got back up to $18 again only on the one hundred and third turn of the wheel, closing at $20 on turn 105 after falling as low as $4 on four different occasions.

Column three hit a high of $35, the highest bet laid in this whole Trilogy game, then came down again. At game's end, when I arbitrarily quit after 105 turns, the progression on the third column was ready to bet $21.

Notice bets Nos. 41, 54 and 96. They're all zeros. All of the columns lost on those bets, and as you can see from table 11.1, it played havoc with the profit column. In a regular game of Two-Step the zeros are scored simply as another loss and don't appear on the balance sheet as anything other than a normal loss, but in Trilogy the zeros are always quite an event, mathematically and emotionally. If you get enough of them in a single game, it'll destroy you.

A Frank Evaluation

I wouldn't play Trilogy in a casino, because it's impossible to play invisibly. Better by far to stick to six different games of Two-Step played on each of the columns and dozens simultaneously, with one bet per progression per table. Trilogy is an interesting system only mathematically; it gives us a chance to consider the bewitching idea of covering every possible outcome at once, just to see what happens. Actually, this everything-at-once approach can be taken yet another step further, and that's by taking the profits from the Trilogy game and using them to finance endless $1 bets on the zero and double-zero, the system described in the next chapter—in other words, Harvesting the Zeros.

Homework

Get your grab bag and try playing Trilogy. In an actual casino you'll be getting in just one bet per column before changing tables, the same way you get in one bet on each of the dozens, plus all the even-money roulette bets before changing tables. It will amount to playing six different games of Two-Step and six of Half Peak, plus all the holistic games in the long-shot center of the layout, which we'll discuss after the next chapter.

12

Harvesting the Zeros

How did the world come to have duplicity in the first place? Children learn it from their parents and so on, but where did it begin? Did early man have these problems?

The Bible says it all began in the Garden of Eden with Adam and Eve tasting the apple, at the snake's behest. Let it be said in their defense, it was a snake whose appearance wasn't against God's will. Did God set them up for a fall? Was it an essential part of human evolution that we all went through this duplicitous phase before moving on?

We may never know fully what happened in the Garden of Eden. All we know for sure is that negativity entered the world, the sky darkened, and suddenly Adam and Eve didn't have it made anymore.

The System Itself

Harvesting the Zeros, like Trilogy, isn't a practical system and is offered here more as a mathematical curiosity, the natural endpoint of the evolution begun in Two-Step and continued in Trilogy. If you're actually out to hedge a roulette wheel, use

86

the system in chapter 25, "The Red-and-Black Hedge." That much said, however, let's consider Harvesting the Zeros.

Mathematical Analysis

A comparison of tables 11.1 and 12.1 serves to illustrate the buffering effect that Harvesting the Zeros has. In table 11.1, the Trilogy game, the extremes of profit run from a low of −$222 in deficit to a high of $78 profit, a $300 range, while in table 12.1, below, the Harvesting the Zeros game, the extremes go from a low of −$31 in deficit to a high of $105 profit, a $136 range, less than half as extreme as the range in the Trilogy game.

Table 12.1
Harvesting the Zeros

AMOUNTS AND DECISIONS
(W = WIN)

BET No.	COL 1	D	COL 2	D	COL 3	D	TOTAL OUT	TOTAL IN	PROFIT
1	$8		$8	W	$8		$26	$24	−$2
2	9	W	6		9		52	51	−1
3	7		7	W	10		78	72	−6
4	8		5	W	11		104	87	−17
5	9		3		12	W	130	123	−7
0	10		4	W	10		156	135	−21
7	11		2		11	W	182	168	−14
8	12		3	W	9		208	177	−31
9	13		1		10	W	234	207	−27
10	14		2		8	W	260	231	−29
11	15	W	3		6		286	276	−10
12	13	00	4	00	7	00	312	311	−1
13	14	W	5		8		341	353	12
14	12	W	6		9		370	389	19
15	10		7		10	W	399	419	20
16	11		8		8	W	428	443	15
17	12	W	9		6		457	479	22
18	10		10		7	W	486	500	14
19	11		11	W	5		515	533	18
20	12		9		6	W	544	551	7

AMOUNTS AND DECISIONS
(W = WIN)

BET No.	COL 1	D	COL 2	D	COL 3	D	TOTAL OUT	TOTAL IN	PROFIT
21	13		10		4	W	573	563	−10
22	14		11	W	2		602	596	−6
23	15	W	9		3		631	641	10
24	13		10		4	W	660	653	−7
25	14	W	11		2		689	695	6
26	12		12	W	3		718	731	13
27	13		10	W	4		747	761	14
28	14	W	8		5		776	803	27
29	12		9		6	W	805	821	16
30	13		10	W	4		834	851	17
31	14	W	8		5		863	893	30
32	12		9	W	6		892	920	28
33	13	W	7		7		921	959	38
34	11	00	8	00	8	00	950	994	44
35	12	W	9		9		982	1,030	48
36	10		10	W	10		1,014	1,060	46
37	11		8	W	11		1,046	1,084	38
38	12	W	6		12		1,078	1,120	42
39	10	W	7		13		1,110	1,150	40
40	8	W	8		14		1,142	1,174	32
41	6	W	9		15		1,174	1,192	18
42	4		10		16	W	1,206	1,240	34
43	5		11		14	W	1,238	1,282	44
44	6		12	W	12		1,270	1,318	48
45	7	W	10		13		1,302	1,339	37
46	5		11	W	14		1,334	1,372	38
47	6	W	9		15		1,366	1,390	24
48	4		10	W	16		1,398	1,420	22
49	5	W	8		17		1,430	1,435	5
50	3	W	9		18		1,462	1,444	−18
51	1		10		19	W	1,494	1,501	7
52	2		11	W	17		1,526	1,534	8
53	3		9	W	18		1,558	1,561	3
54	4		7		19	W	1,590	1,618	28
55	5		8	W	17		1,622	1,642	20
56	6	W	6		18		1,654	1,660	6
57	4	W	7		19		1,686	1,672	−14
58	2		8		20	W	1,718	1,732	14
59	3		9		18	W	1,750	1,786	36
60	4		10		16	W	1,782	1,834	52
61	5		11	W	14		1,814	1,867	53

BET No.	COL 1	D	COL 2	D	COL 3	D	TOTAL OUT	TOTAL IN	PROFIT
62	6	W	9		15		1,846	1,885	39
63	4		10		16	W	1,878	1,933	55
64	5		11		14	W	1,910	1,975	65
65	6	W	12		12		1,942	1,993	51
66	4	0	13	0	13	0	1,974	2,028	54
67	4	W	14		14		2,009	2,043	34
68	3		15		15	W	2,044	2,088	44
69	4		16		13	W	2,079	2,127	48
70	5		17	W	11		2,114	2,178	64
71	6		15	W	12		2,149	2,223	74
72	7		13		13	W	2,184	2,262	78
73	8	0	14	0	11	0	2,219	2,297	78
74	9		15		12	W	2,257	2,333	76
75	10		16	W	10		2,295	2,381	86
76	11	W	14		11		2,333	2,414	81
77	$9		$15		$12	W	$2,371	$2,450	$79

To understand all this, and why zero harvesting works the way it does, let's take a look at the numbers.

A Trilogy game consists of three simultaneous games of Two-Step. If each Two-Step game produces a theoretical profit of $1 (or one unit) on every turn of the wheel, then a Trilogy game produces a theoretical profit of $3 (or three units) on every turn of the wheel. The essence of zero harvesting is to forgo $2 of that $3 profit and spend the $2 instead, placing $1 bets each on zero and double zero. This way the Trilogy part of the game is theoretically earning only $1 on each turn of the wheel but it's making it possible for you to bet zero and double-zero *for free* on every turn of the wheel. Thus you're eligible to get a beautiful 35-to-1 payoff every time either a zero or a double-zero shows up on the wheel. On average this should be once in every nineteen turns. Fewer than that, you end up losing money. More than that, you end up making a nice profit.

If this sort of hedging should ever get you barred from a casino, you might want to let the press know.

The game charted out in table 12.1 has no extremes of luck either way. It won a mere $79 and was so solidly hedged it never went more than –$31 into deficit. The middle column was the theoretical big loser in this example, but in absolute terms it didn't lose anything, it just happened to be $9 above its starting point when I called it quits.

The middle column would have begun to win eventually had I hung in long enough. In fact, it hadn't even risen far enough up the scale yet to qualify for half peak. It started at $8, which meant it would have had to go all the way to $21 to establish $10.50 or $11 as a valid half peak.

The other two columns did considerably better. The third column went to a high of $20, coming to rest ultimately at $12 on turn No. 77.

A Frank Evaluation

Harvesting the Zeros is a theoretically interesting system, but it's utterly impractical and I wouldn't consider trying to make it work in real life. If you like roulette, I recommend the holistic systems, played invisibly. I'll be getting to them next. Either that or, if you're with a partner, the roulette hedging system in chapter 25, once again, the Red-and-Black Hedge. It's designed to zero in on one of the fundamental weaknesses of the roulette layout, an irregularity in the distribution of colors, a mistake someone made back when roulette was first invented.

13

Holistic Roulette I

Why would someone zap someone else with hate? It happens all the time. It's a common experience of life. Why on earth would someone do it in the first place? My hunch is that someone else may have done it to *them* in childhood.

It's unfortunately true that if we carry the pain of hatred within us we can relieve ourselves of some of the burden by injecting someone else with it. It's only temporary relief, but for the brief time it lasts the relief is genuine enough, so people end up injecting others with hate, not realizing they're polluting *everybody's* spiritual environment, and not realizing God is testing them, giving them a chance to hate just to see if they will or not—a very heavy test and a tragedy to fail.

In a sense it's like a vast spiritual inflammation that the whole human race is suffering from. It would seem that the first step ought to be merely to wake everybody up to what's happening, get them all to agree to change, and be however patient they need to be with one another during that period of change to get the inflammation quelled.

Would that work? Somehow you know it just wouldn't. So what is the problem? What's the key to getting the information quelled?

The problem is a non-material but real entity called Satan. Liberals will laugh, I know, but I'm not referring to a devil with a pointy tail and horns. I mean a voice in your mind. Everybody has voices in their mind, don't they? Not just Joan of Arc, although she certainly made more of her voices than most people make of theirs. Maybe voice is the wrong word, since it's not so much a voice as a verbal thought, a feeling, something felt rather than actually heard. We all think to ourselves, is what I mean. It's how thinking is done. Who exactly are these many voices participating in these all-important thought conversations which decide our behavior? We experience them as being inside our head so there's an understandable tendency to conclude that they must be a part of us, and therefore to regard them as fully reliable. They are on our side and benign in every way. How could they not be benign, being a part of us, right?

People who were lucky enough to get early religious training know better. They know that at least one of these voices is something called Satan. He's real in spite of being non-material and he's not part of you at all, no more than a wart is part of you, in spite of the illusion of his appearing to be located inside your mind. Don't be so sure you know what the inside of your mind consists of. Scientists and mathematicians know about higher dimensionalities that human senses can't grasp. Just as medieval man couldn't grasp how the earth could be round, so-called modern man has trouble grasping how a voice could be inside him and yet not be a part of him.

In most every mathematician's education and training he runs across a Victorian tale called *Flatland,* by Edwin Abbott, a story about life in a two-dimensional world with a whole culture and civilization existing in two dimensions. People there are triangles, squares, pentagons, and so on—every kind of polygon. The more sides you have, the higher is your class status in the culture of that two-dimensional world. The aristocrats are the people with so many sides they start to look like circles.

Someone from our world could see inside the head of a resident of Flatland, and if he represented himself as being reliably a part of that two-dimensional person by reason of his being located inside that two-dimensional person's head, would he be able to fool a Flatlander?

He would if he studied Flatlander's minds for a long, long time and was wise in the subject of Flatlander nature, knowing what they believe, what they don't believe, what they go for and what they can be persuaded to go for.

In Satan's case there's the additional aspect that he also makes a living from this whole fantastic process. Every time he succeeds in getting you to do something that causes your vessel to become smaller you lose aura, the glow of living things. Your face glows a little less brightly. The lost aura has now gone to Satan instead. *He* glows more brightly now, and at your expense. This aura is what they use for money in heaven. Every time you agree to diminish yourself in response to the suggestion of a voice in your mind you make Satan richer. He then glows that much more brightly and as a result, the next time that little voice in your mind offers a suggestion, the voice will be a teensy bit louder.

The System Itself

Okay now, here's the roulette system for you. Approaching a roulette wheel today (openly, not invisibly), knowing what I know about the various roulette systems in this book, the system I'd play is the one coming up here.

Holistic Roulette is actually four separate systems, all kissing cousins of one another. It's probably the best general approach to roulette, offering four different levels of risk. If you're a wise and cautious player, you'll choose the least risky of them. If you're a more adventurous type, you can choose the level of risk it takes to make your stomach do butterflies. The least risky is the six-number system. Between Half Peak and Two-Step we've already learned quite a few ways to place bets on the roulette layout, but there are more sophisticated ways to beat a roulette table that we haven't looked at yet, *all* of them strong additional profit centers if you choose the invisibility mode.

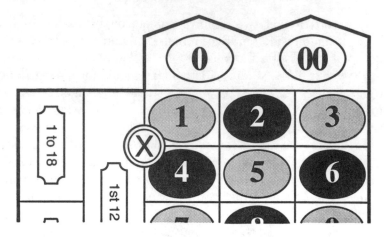

Fig. 13.1. The Six-Number Bet

The first of these more sophisticated ways is the six-number bet, betting six adjacent inside numbers at once. If the ball lands on any of the six, you win, paying 5 to 1. The true odds are 5.33 to 1, not a bad spread, only about 6.667 percent edge for the house. Compare it, for example, with the 1-to-1 bets on the roulette table, which take a 4.4 percent edge but pay only 1 to 1, utterly nowhere compared to the kinds of multiplication possibilities inherent in a high-leverage 5-to-1 payoff.

The way to place a six-number bet is to bet two rows at once. They can be any two rows as long as they're side by side. Place your chips on the line between the two rows but on the near edge of the inside. On the layout shown in fig. 13.1, for example, if you put a chip covering the lower left corner of number 25 and the upper left corner of number 28, it means you're betting all six numbers in both rows: 25, 26, 27, 28, 29, and 30, all from that one chip. (If you wanted to bet just 25 and 28, you would slide the chip away from the corners and center it on the line between 25 and 28.)

Likewise, if you place a chip covering the lower left corner of number 1 and the upper left corner of number 4, you'd be betting on all six of the numbers in both those rows: 1, 2, 3, 4, 5, and 6. If any of them came in, you'd win five times the amount of your bet, plus you'd get your bet back, equal therefore to six times the amount you parted with before the tourneur spun the wheel.

To begin a six-number Holistic Roulette progression you open with a bet of $1 and keep increasing by $1 after every loss until you win, then decrease the bet by $7 to create the necessary drift downward. I know that in craps we always decided the correction factor by adding 2 to the true odds, but here that would hurt too much because it is only a true 6 to 1, which means not enough leverage. Correcting by only $7 is riskier (12.5 percent less drift downward) but 6-to-1 odds are low-risk enough to compensate, please Lord. The game ends when you get back down to $1. At that point you either total up your winnings and celebrate or press your luck further, as the spirit moves you.

Now there's a hitch here, unfortunately, but only for visible players. For invisible players it's no problem. The hitch is that the house won't let you bet just $1, as they will at craps. The house minimum at roulette is always going to be at least $2 and much more likely $3, so when you go to plunk down the first $1 bet the dealer is going to stop you and say, "Sorry, but there's a three-dollar minimum." This is a regrettable truth of roulette, but it's understandable because the house really isn't claiming that much of an edge here, only 6.667 percent on a bet that pays 5 to 1. (Remember that the 7 on the craps table pays 4 to 1, one less than the 6-number bet at roulette, but there the house is claiming a 20 percent edge. So you can see the difference: in craps, where the payout isn't even as good, the house cuts itself three times as big a slice.)

Even the class houses are this way, alas, so it won't do you any good to go shopping around. The $3 minimum is part of the price the system player is expected to pay for the privilege of playing up against so narrow a house edge. But in a class house, happily, there's a nice loophole you can use to get around the minimum. It's called dividing your bet: the $3 minimum doesn't apply to any given bet, it applies to any given turn of the wheel. The house doesn't care where on the inside you place your $3, whether you put it all on one bet or divide it among two or three bets, provided you've got a total of at least $3 riding on any given turn of the wheel. Three dollars per turn of the wheel is what the house charges you to sit at the table and play, in other words, but it's up to you to decide how to spend that $3—all in one place or in two or three different places.

For the invisible player who's betting only one bet in each progression at each wheel in the house, it's easy to do two or more inside progressions at once. (The others could be Holistic Roulette II and Holistic Roulette III.) This easily covers any minimum.

Plus there's another approach that's even easier. It's called the mad money approach. You just figure out how much extra you're going to need to meet the minimum and declare that extra to be mad money, money to be bet in a crazy, illogical way, solely according to impulse. Then, on the second turn, when the next bet in the progression is $2, just toss a single $1 chip out onto the layout to bring the bet up to a minimum. If it were a $5 minimum, you'd have to sprinkle that many more chips around, until your progression at last reached $5.

Mathematical Analysis

Table 13.1
Six-Number Holistic Roulette

Bet No.	Amount	Decision	Total Out	Total In	Profit
1	$1	L	$1		-$1
2	2	L	3		-3
3	3	L	6		-6
4	4	L	10		-10
5	5	L	15		-15
6	6	W	21	$36	15
7	1	L	22		14
8	2	L	24		12

Bet No.	Amount	Decision	Total Out	Total In	Profit
9	3	L	27		9
10	4	W	31	60	29
11	1	L	32		28
12	2	L	34		26
13	3	L	37		23
14	4	L	41		19
15	5	L	46		14
16	6	L	52		8
17	7	L	59		1
18	8	L	67		−7
19	9	L	76		−16
20	10	L	86		−26
21	11	L	97		−37
22	12	L	109		−49
23	13	L	122		−62
24	14	W	136	144	8
25	7	W	143	186	43
26	1	L	144		42
27	2	L	146		40
28	3	W	149	204	55
29	1	L	150		54
30	2	L	152		52
31	3	L	155		49
32	4	L	159		45
33	5	L	164		40
34	6	L	170		34
35	7	L	177		27
36	8	W	185	252	67
37	1	L	186		66
38	2	L	188		64
39	3	L	191		61
40	4	W	195	276	81
41	1	L	196		80
42	2	W	198	288	90
43	1	W	199	294	95
44	1	W	200	300	100
45	2	L	202		98
46	3	L	205		95
47	4	L	209		91
48	5	L	214		86
49	6	L	220		80
50	7	L	227		73
51	8	L	235		65
52	9	L	244		56

Bet No.	Amount	Decision	Total Out	Total In	Profit
53	10	L	254		46
54	11	L	265		35
55	12	L	277		23
56	13	L	290		10
57	14	W	304		80
58	$7	W	$311		$115
(59)	(1)				

The mad money approach is the one I used in the six-number Holistic Roulette game shown in table 13.1. On each of the $1 and $2 bets shown in the sample game, I was hypothetically obliged to pony up an extra one or two chips to stay legal.

Thus table 13.1 begins with a bet of $1, in spite of the $3 minimum. Thank heaven for loopholes. From $1 I worked my way up to $6 before winning, and this turned a $15 deficit into a $15 profit. I immediately returned to $1 and started the progression over again. After another win on bet No. 10, I hit a moderate losing streak and tumbled yet another –$62 into deficit, my low for the game, before winning the twenty-fourth turn, a bet of $14 which brought in 5 × $14 = $70 plus my $14 bet itself, neatly eliminating the deficit and leaving me an $8 profit besides.

Then something nice happened: I won bet No. 25 as well, the very next turn of the wheel. Suddenly, in the space of two turns of the wheel, I jumped from –$62 in deficit to $43 profit. This can be exhilarating, but you have to keep a clear head on these matters and realize it's only the probabilistic flip side of all those times you lose two or three dozen in a row.

From then on it was just your standard game of nail-biting Holistic Roulette. I worked my way back to $55 profit on turn No. 28 before working my way back down to only $27 on turn No. 35, but then by turn No. 44 I was up to a solid $100 profit again.

By turn No. 56 the $100 profit had melted back to a mere $10, reminding me of the wise advice, "Quit while you're ahead," but on turn No. 57 I hit another nice winner, a bet of $14 paying $70 profit and the progression was back up to $80 ahead. The following $7 bet won, and the total profit jumped back up to $115, a nice haul for about an hour's worth of play on a relatively low-risk game, as you can see. Sure, you could stay all night and maybe win a zillion dollars, but you might lose the $115 and go home with nothing. A hundred and fifteen dollars is much less than a zillion dollars, but it's still a lot more than zero. This is called common sense, and it's an indispensable part of any successful system player's mental equipment. Make sure you don't leave yours home.

If you're playing six-number Holistic Roulette, you don't have to keep betting the same six-numbers turn after turn. You can keep jumping around from one set of six to another all over the inside. It doesn't change anything mathematically—your chances are still exactly the same as when you stick with the same six numbers turn after turn—but jumping your bet around gives you the chance to play your hunches at the same time you play your progression. Whether you want to do this or not depends on how much faith you have in your hunches. If you're the kind who frets over might-have-beens, you might do better just to stick with the same six numbers all night, although you can fret just as well over not having changed your numbers as you can over having changed them.

A Frank Evaluation

Holistic Roulette works marvelously at home. In the casino you're going to be astonished at how many more zeros come up. My hunch is, the best way is just to learn the invisibility method right from the start, in which case your progression in the six-number bet at roulette is just another of the many you're tracking in that secret notebook you'll be carrying around.

Homework

Play a game of Holistic Roulette I, a progression on the six-number bet, just like the one in table 13.1. See how much you win. Note once again the lengths of your losing streaks so you can compare them with Holistic Roulette II, III and IV.

14

Holistic Roulette II

Besides the six-number bet at roulette there's also something called the five-number bet, but this is located at only one spot on the inside and you can't jump it around as with the six-number bet.

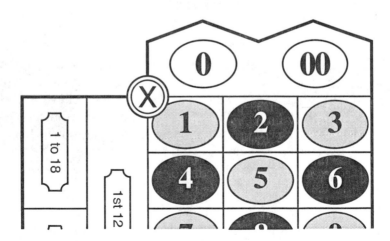

Fig. 14.1. The Five-Number Bet

The System Itself

The five numbers in the five-number bet are 0, 00, 1, 2 and 3, and only these five, as shown by letter X in fig. 14.1. You bet it by placing your chips covering the upper left-hand corner of number 1 and the lower left-hand corner of number 0. The payoff is 6 to 1 against true odds of 6.6 to 1, or roughly a 10.99 percent edge for the house. By itself this isn't as favorable as the six-number bet, but five-number Holistic Roulette can be played as a hedge when any run has a high number of 0's and 00's. It yields a nice profit to counterbalance losses that these zeros tend to cause in a Two-Step game. Correct by $7.

A Frank Analysis

If you suspect the house to be using a crooked wheel and sending out extra zeros, then obviously the five-number bet is the One True Way.

Other than as a hedge, the five-number game is just an intermediary between the six-number game and the four-number game. If the six-number bet is too conservative for you, then the next step up is the five-number bet. Either that or the four-number bet, the next Holistic Roulette system we're going to look at.

Homework

Play a game of Holistic Roulette II, a progression on the five-number bet. Once again, log your highs, lows, and lengths of losing streaks in order to compare them with the other forms of Holistic Roulette.

15

Holistic Roulette III

So we're back to square one again, how do we defeat Satan? If he's the cause of the spiritual inflammation that's afflicting the human race and the goal is to quell that inflammation, how do we go about it?

Step one, once again, would seem to be to alert everyone to the matter, but the problem is that a little voice in their minds is likely to say, "Nice idea, but it won't work."

You see, Satan can introduce more than mere verbal suggestions, he can also introduce feelings. One of his favorites is doubt.

That voice in your mind, be it Satan or whoever, sees and hears your every thought. It knows you well. You, on the other hand, what do *you* know about it? Satan's greatest victory is getting you to believe he doesn't really exist. Once he does that, he's got you. From then on he can suggest absolutely anything, no matter how preposterous, and you will never know to be cautious.

What it would take to defeat Satan would be to find a way to both wake everyone up and to motivate them to work together once they were awake to (1) cut off his nurture and then (2) alter the wrong habits of the human race in order to keep that nurture cut off. Then his glow would fade and his voice would become steadily fainter until at least future generations reached a point where he's not a part of their lives anymore.

Could this happen?

The System Itself

Satan aside for the moment, you may recall in the discussion of Baby Hardways I talked at some length about the real-world difference between true odds of 8 to 1 and true odds of 10 to 1. It doesn't seem like much of a difference superficially, but that little bit can mean a great deal more grief when you run into bad luck. True odds of 10 to 1 seem to be only 25 percent riskier than true odds of 8 to 1, but the difference in real life can be staggering. A longer shot is that much harder to win in the best of circumstances, and in the worst of circumstances it can become an absolute nightmare. You're standing there waiting for a number to appear that's only remotely likely to appear in the first place.

The difference between long shots and longer shots isn't measured in the best of times, it's measured in the worst of times, and this is what you have to consider before you sit down

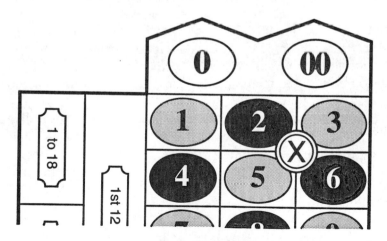

Fig. 15.1. The Four-Number Bet

to play a progression on a longer shot. It's no real difference as long as you run into reasonable luck, but heaven help you if you run into unreasonable luck, which happens, pal, believe it.

Table 15.1 provides a fine, real-life example of just what I'm talking about. This is a more advanced Holistic Roulette system called the four-number system.

Mathematical Analysis

You learned two chapters ago how to place a six-number bet and cover all the numbers in two adjacent rows at once. Well, there's also a four-number bet. It pays 8 to 1, not 5 to 1, the payoff of the 6-number bet. There you see the difference. The gap between 5 to 1 and 8 to 1 can seem like a canyon sometimes. The true odds on the 8 to 1 bets are 8.5 to 1, giving the house a 6.25 percent edge, slightly narrower than the 6.667 percent they were taking on the six-number bet. But beware—you're sticking your neck out quite a bit further by jumping from a 5 to 1 to an 8 to 1.

Still, if you want the higher profit potential that an 8 to 1 payoff provides and you don't mind the extra risk, the way to place a four-number bet is to put your chips down squarely on the intersection of the four numbers you want to bet, as shown by letter X in fig. 15.1. They have to be four adjacent numbers. It's not like some of the state lottery games where you get to pick any numbers you like. Not that this really makes any difference: the mathematics (odds) are exactly the same no matter which four numbers you bet.

A progression in four-number Holistic Roulette starts like any other, with a $1 bet. Once again there's the house minimum to contend with, but as before you just make whatever mad money bets you need to bring your total wager for that run of the wheel up to the minimum. If you're stuck at a $5 wheel, you can cover more than half the numbers on the table making five $1 bets on that first turn and stand a reasonable chance of winning a nice 8-to-1 payoff.

Table 15.1
Four-Number Holistic Roulette

Bet No.	Amount	Decision	Total Out	Total In	Profit
1	$1	W	$1	$9	$8
2	1	L	2		7
3	2	L	4		5
4	3	L	7		2
5	4	W	11	45	34
6	1	L	12		33
7	2	L	14		31
8	3	W	17	72	55
9	1	L	18		54
10	2	L	20		52
11	3	L	23		49
12	4	L	32		40
13	5	L	32		40
14	6	L	38		34
15	7	L	45		27
16	8	L	53		19
17	9	L	62		10
18	10	L	72		0
19	11	L	83		−11
20	12	L	95		−23
21	13	L	108		−36
22	14	L	122		−50
23	15	L	137		−65
24	16	L	153		−81
25	17	L	170		−98
26	18	L	188		−116
27	19	L	207		−135
28	20	L	227		−155
29	21	L	248		−176
30	22	L	270		−198
31	23	L	293		−221
32	24	L	317		−245
33	25	L	342		−270
34	26	L	368		−296
35	27	L	395		−323
36	28	L	423		−351
37	29	L	452		−380
38	30	L	482		−410
39	31	L	513		−441
40	32	L	545		−473

Bet No.	Amount	Decision	Total Out	Total In	Profit
4133	W	578	369	−209	
42	23	L	601		−232
43	24	L	625		−256
44	25	L	650		−281
45	26	L	676		−307
46	27	L	703		−334
47	28	L	731		−362
48	29	W	760	630	−130
49	19	L	779		−149
50	20	L	799		−169
51	21	W	820	819	−1
52	11	L	831		−12
53	12	L	843		−24
54	13	L	856		−37
55	14	L	870		−51
56	15	L	885		−66
57	16	L	901		−82
58	17	L	918		−99
59	18	L	936		−117
60	19	L	955		−136
61	20	L	975		−156
62	21	L	996		−177
63	22	L	1,018		−199
64	23	L	1,041		−222
65	24	L	1,065		−246
66	25	L	1,090		−271
67	26	W	1,116	1,053	−63
68	16	W	1,132	1,197	65
69	6	L	1,138		59
70	7	L	1,145		52
71	8	L	1,153		44
72	9	L	1,162		35
73	10	L	1,172		25
74	11	L	1,183		14
75	12	L	1,195		2
76	13	L	1,208		−11
77	14	L	1,222		−25
78	15	W	1,237	1,332	95
79	5	L	1,242		90
80	6	L	1,248		84
81	7	L	1,255		77
82	8	L	1,263		69
83	9	L	1,272		60
84	10	L	1,282		50

BET No.	Amount	Decision	Total Out	Total In	Profit
85	11	L	1,293		39
86	12	L	1,305		27
87	13	L	1,318		14
88	14	L	1,332		0
89	15	L	1,347		−15
90	16	W	1,363	1,476	113
91	6	L	1,369		107
92	7	L	1,376		100
93	8	L	1,384		92
94	$9	W	$1,393	$1,557	$164
(95)	(1)				

Table 15.1 is a four-number Holistic Roulette game. It will illustrate my point about risk very nicely. As you can see from the chart, at one point I was −$473 in the hole. This was on bet No. 40 after a thoroughly sobering streak of *thirty-two losses in a row*. That's the sort of thing you have to contend with on long shots like 8 to 1. With the more docile 5-to-1 odds on the 6-number progression it's fairly rare to drop thirty-two in a row, but with the hairier 8 to 1 you can run into this sort of thing all too readily. This is why I'm always so skittish about playing the hard 6 or hard 8 when I'm playing the Hardways at craps. The hard 6 and hard 8 are 9-to-1 payouts, even riskier than the four-number bets at roulette at only 8 to 1. The hard 4 and hard 10, by contrast, are less risky at only 7 to 1, although even 7 to 1 can really dish out the heartburn on a bad night.

The game in table 15.1 finally started to climb its way back out of the hole by turn No. 67, which was a bet of $26. I corrected by $10, since it's an 8 to 1, to create a welcome drift downward. Then something improbable happened. I won again at $16. Two wins in a row on an 8-to-1 shot! This corrected the bet down from $26 to only $6, and the game was finally showing a profit again, although only a modest $65. From there it went and worked itself back down into a hole again, getting down to −$25 in deficit before rising suddenly back up to what was at that point a new high for the game, $95. Then the whole $95 disappeared, plus another –$15 of deficit. On turn No. 90 I won again. By then my progression was all the way up to $16 again, so the winnings at 8 × $16 launched me right back into the profit zone, with $113 to show for my time and trouble. On turn No. 94, when I stopped, I had a nice $164 profit overall.

A Frank Evaluation

In this case I got lucky, but it could have turned out otherwise. Eight to one is a whole lot longer a long shot than 5 to 1. When browsing through table 15.1, pay more attention to the –$473 deficit than the $164 profit overall. That'll give you a much clearer picture of reality.

Homework

Try your luck with a progression on the four-number bet. See how you do. Compare and contrast it with the five-number and six-number bets, the highs, lows, lengths of longest and second-longest losing streaks.

16

Holistic Roulette IV

Spiritual pollution in the end is largely just a matter of bad habits created and cultivated in the human race by Satan over thousands of years and passed along from one generation to the next. It would appear then that it really is possible to get our spiritual environment cleaned up, but only by our being willing to expend the tremendous energy needed to make changes in habits of long standing. Would that really be possible? How would we go about it? Where would we begin?

The idea of landing a man on the moon once seemed as utterly fantastic as communication with the dead. And yet a committed nation undertook this project and succeeded. No doubt God had many different reasons for allowing the Apollo program to succeed, but at least one of them, surely, was to teach us to have confidence in ourselves.

The System Itself

Now after the whole discussion in the last chapter about the perils of an 8 to 1 instead of a 5 to 1, I'm sure I don't have to dwell at length about what kind of situation you're up against with an 11 to 1 or a 17 to 1, but that's what we're going to look at in this chapter, the three-number bet and, Lord be with you, the two-number bet. If you're using the invisibility method and betting only one bet on each progression per table, drop the three- and two-number bets because you won't have roulette wheels enough to pull it off. Just leave them out of that secret little notebook of yours.

The basic Holistic Roulette system is an extremely flexible one. Just as you can build progressions on the six-number, five-number, and four-number bets, you can build them on the three-number and two-number bets as well. It's all just a matter of risk. Take as much as you want, since the house is most agreeable on this score.

Risk makes both these systems unrealistic. Still, they're worth looking at just for the sake of knowing about them and how they work, and what this can teach you about roulette and very long odds.

To place a three-number bet you must bet an entire row of three at once. (A row is the opposite of a column, remember.) It's very similar to betting the six-number bet except that instead of betting two rows at once you're betting only one row. You place your chips on the line marking off the near edge of the inside, as in the six-number bet, but instead of centering the chips between the lower left hand corner of the upper row and the upper left hand corner of the lower row, you center them on the left edge number in the row you want to bet. By placing your chips on the left edge of the number instead of squarely on the number you indicate a bet on the entire row instead of only one number. In gambling slang it's a "street bet." Letter X in fig. 16.1 illustrates a street bet on numbers 7, 8, and 9, for example.

Mathematical Analysis

Both progressions start at $1, as in all the Holistic Roulette games. Then, if you lose, you keep increasing the bet by $1

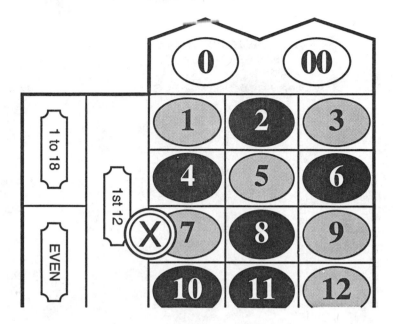

Fig. 16.1. The Three-Number Bet

until you win, then you reduce your bet just enough to create a mathematical drift downward, For a three-number progression at 11 to 1 you correct by $13 after each win. For a two-number progression at 17 to 1 you correct by $20 after each win, decreasing by $3, not $2, to increase the rate of the drift downward. The true odds on the 11 to 1 are 11.667 to one, giving the house a 6.06 percent edge. The true odds on the 17 to 1 are 18 to 1, giving the house a 5.882 percent edge.

Note well that the house edge on the four-number bet in the last chapter is only 6.25 percent and on the six-number bet (two chapters before) only 6.667 percent. From the six-number bet to the two-number bet the house edge decreases *by less than one percent*. This is why I am so wary of the longer-odds bets. You're not really getting that much more of a bargain on the longer-odds bets, yet the risk increases dramatically.

Table 16.1
Three-Number Holistic Roulette

Bet No.	Amount	Decision	Total Out	Total In	Profit
1	$1	L	$1		$-31
2	2	L	3		-3
3	3	L	6		-6
4	4	L	10		-10
5	5	L	15		-15
6	6	L	21		-21
7	7	L	28		-28
8	8	L	36		-36
9	9	L	45		-45
10	10	L	55		-55
11	11	L	66		-66
12	12	L	78		-78
13	13	L	91		-91
14	14	L	105		-105
15	15	L	120		-120
16	16	L	136		-136
17	17	L	153		-153
18	18	L	171		-171
19	19	L	190		-190
20	20	L	210		-210
21	21	W	231	$252	21
22	8	L	239		13
23	9	L	248		4
24	10	L	258		-6
25	11	L	269		-17
26	12	L	281		-29
27	13	L	294		-42
28	14	L	308		-56
29	15	L	323		-71
30	16	L	339		-87
31	17	L	356		-104
32	18	L	374		-122
33	19	L	393		-141
34	20	L	413		-161
35	21	L	434		-182
36	22	L	456		-204
37	23	L	479		-227
38	24	L	503		-251
39	25	W	528	552	24
40	12	L	540		12

Bet No.	Amount	Decision	Total Out	Total In	Profit
41	13	L	553		−1
42	14	L	567		−15
43	15	L	582		−30
44	16	W	598	744	146
45	3	W	601	780	179
46	1	L	602		178
47	2	L	604		176
48	3	L	607		173
49	4	L	611		169
50	$5	L	$616		$164
(51)	(6)				

Table 16.2
Two-Number Holistic Roulette

Bet No.	Amount	Decision	Total Out	Total In	Profit
1	$1	L	$1		−$1
2	2	L	3		−3
3	3	L	6		−6
4	4	L	10		−10
5	5	L	15		−15
6	6	L	21		−21
7	7	L	28		−28
8	8	L	36		−36
9	9	L	45		−45
10	10	L	55		−55
11	11	L	66		−66
12	12	L	78		−78
13	13	L	91		−91
14	14	L	105		−105
15	15	L	120		−120
16	16	L	136		−136
17	17	L	153		−153
18	18	L	171		−171
19	19	L	190		−190
20	20	L	210		−210
21	21	L	231		−231
22	22	L	253		−253
23	23	L	276		−276
24	24	L	300		−300
25	25	L	325		−325

Bet No.	Amount	Decision	Total Out	Total In	Profit
26	26	L	351		−351
27	27	L	378		−378
28	28	L	406		−406
29	29	L	435		−435
30	30	W	465	540	75
31	11	L	476		64
32	12	L	488		52
33	13	L	501		39
34	14	L	515		25
35	15	L	530		10
36	16	L	546		−6
37	17	L	563		−23
38	18	W	581	864	283
39	1	L	582		282
40	2	L	584		280
41	3	L	587		277
42	4	L	591		273
43	5	L	596		268
44	6	L	602		262
45	7	L	609		255
46	8	L	617		247
47	9	L	626		238
48	10	L	636		228
49	11	L	647		217
50	12	L	659		205
51	13	L	672		192
52	14	L	686		178
53	15	L	701		163
54	16	L	717		147
55	$17	W	$734	$1,170	$436

The game in table 16.1 was a lucky one. You can see from the chart that in spite of its being a lucky game it sank a full −$210 into deficit *before winning a thing,* and even then the winnings were enough only to cover the losses. In fact, until the forty-fourth turn of the wheel, the third win, it hadn't yet made a dime off forty-three turns. Worse than that, the deficit on turn No. 38 had sunk to what later turned out to be a game low of −$251, and all this before showing even one dollar of profit. Do you see what I mean about the hazards of playing long shots? And table 16.1, I say again, was a lucky game.

From there, however, things brightened. The progression won two in a row on bets No. 44 and No. 45 and finally showed a profit. Technically the game had ended at that point since the bet had worked its way back down to zero, but I wanted to keep going, and later quit with a total game profit of $164.

Table 16.2 is a two-number game. It lost twenty-nine turns in a row and sank more than $400 in the hole before it finally won one. These are thought-provoking numbers, believe it. But note what happened when it finally won a single bet: the entire −$435 deficit vanished immediately and was replaced by a $75 profit. All that from one bet.

The math here is worth looking at. Every time we lost we raised the bet by $1. By the time we lost twenty-nine in a row the bet was up to $30. But when that $30 won at 17 to 1 (plus the $30 itself) we suddenly raked in a virtual landslide of chips, $540 worth, all from a single spin of the wheel. This of course is what makes the heavy long shots attractive—not the risk, but the awesome profit potential inherent in any bet with a very, very high payoff. Wall Street calls this leverage, but that's actually just a fancy term for sticking your neck out.

After that first win the bet fell to $11 and rose up to $18 before winning again. On the second win, on bet No. 38, the tremendous impact of a 17-to-1 payoff once again became clear. After turn No. 37 we were −$23 in the hole again. After turn No. 38 we suddenly had a $283 profit. Then we lost sixteen in a row before winning again on turn No. 55, a bet of $17, as you can see from table 16.2. The payoff was 17 × $17 = $289, plus the $17 bet, making $306 in all. The total profit for the game was $436.

A Frank Evaluation

If you want to get started with the two-number bets, the way to do it is simple. First you have your doctor write you a prescription for a good, strong tranquilizer, then pick any two adjacent numbers and lay your chips down right in the center of the line between them. In gambling slang this is called a "split." The double meaning becomes clear when you become schizophrenic watching all your money go down the drain.

I would never play a game this risky except with somebody else's money, and even then I would worry the wheel might be wired.

If you stick to the six-number bet, roulette isn't all that risky, but my warning about the longer shots must stand, especially the three-number and two-number bets. You may very well win at home but your luck will change in the casinos. Why? I don't know why. I merely report the fact for people to mull over. There could be any number of legitimate explanations for this mystery. Don't assume the tables are wired.

Homework

Compare and contrast, as always. The idea is to play every system at least once for the sake of first-hand experience—even the impossibly risky ones.

17

Lucky Number

The good news is that the loudness of Satan's voice, varying over time, is getting steadily weaker. Within the span of a single human lifetime the change has not been generally noticeable. The future may be different, however, as a quantum shift takes place when the last of the spiritual pollution has been cleaned up.

What this means is that Satan's time is running out. The inflammation is subsiding and a great new golden age is coming.

The System Itself

There's actually one other approach to Holistic Roulette, but this one is so extreme it can't really be called Holistic Roulette anymore. It's called Lucky Number and it is, hands down, absolutely the last word in risk, even worse than Tailspin. My honest advice to you is that you consider this system in theory only.

So far we've seen systems designed to accommodate the six-number bet, five-number bet, four-number bet, three-number

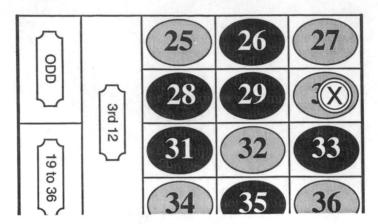

Fig. 17.1 Lucky Number

bet and two-number bet. The trend here is so obvious that the question begs to be asked: is there a system designed for the one-number or straight bet? There is indeed. Lucky Number is based on the 35-to-1 long shot. Theoretically it's the most profitable of all casino systems, which is its appeal, as you'll see on table 17.1.

Mathematical Analysis

The first thing you'll note from table 17.1 is that we lost forty-five bets in a row before winning anything. That adds up to $1,035 plunked down before we raked in so much as a dime. And that wasn't even such a bad losing streak by Lucky Number standards. We could easily have run through a hundred bets or more before winning anything, in which case we'd have been *more than five thousand dollars in the hole*. And yet, when we won, what happened? We won 35 × $46 = $1,610, plus the $46 wager itself. Which equals $1,656, a $575 profit.

Table 17.1
Lucky Number

Bet No.	Amount	Decision	Total Out	Total In	Profit
1	$1	L	$1		-$1
2	2	L	3		-3
3	3	L	6		-6
4	4	L	10		-10
5	5	L	15		-15
6	6	L	21		-21
7	7	L	28		-28
8	8	L	36		-36
9	9	L	45		-45
10	10	L	55		-55
11	11	L	66		-66
12	12	L	78		-78
13	13	L	91		-91
14	14	L	105		-105
15	15	L	120		-120
16	16	L	136		-136
17	17	L	153		-153
18	18	L	171		-171
19	19	L	190		-190
20	20	L	210		-210
21	21	L	231		-231
22	22	L	253		-253
23	23	L	276		-276
24	24	L	300		-300
25	25	L	325		-325
26	26	L	351		-351
27	27	L	378		-378
28	28	L	406		-406
29	29	L	435		-435
30	30	L	465		-465
31	31	L	496		-496
32	32	L	528		-528
33	33	L	561		-561
34	34	L	595		-595
35	35	L	630		-630
36	36	L	666		-666
37	37	L	703		-703
38	38	L	741		-741
39	39	L	780		-780

Bet No.	Amount	Decision	Total Out	Total In	Profit
40	40	L	820		−820
41	41	L	861		−861
42	42	L	903		−903
43	43	L	946		−946
44	44	L	990		−990
45	45	L	1,035		−1,035
46	46	W	1,081	$1,650	575
47	7	L	1,088		568
48	8	L	1,096		560
49	9	L	1,105		551
50	10	L	1,115		541
51	11	L	1,126		530
52	12	L	1,138		518
53	13	L	1,151		505
54	14	L	1,165		491
55	15	L	1,180		476
56	16	L	1,196		460
57	17	L	1,213		443
58	18	L	1,231		425
59	19	L	1,250		406
60	20	L	1,270		386
61	21	L	1,291		365
62	22	L	1,313		343
63	23	L	1,336		320
64	24	L	1,360		296
65	25	L	1,385		271
66	$26	W	$1,411	$2,592	$1,181

We corrected by $39 again and placed a bet of $7, then worked our way back up to $26, ultimately, before winning one last time. The total profit for the entire series of turns was $1,181, and all this came from *just two wins*.

A Frank Evaluation

Like the other fantasy systems in this book, including the next one, Lucky Number is for contemplation only. This is no simple Hardways or easy holistic progression, this is *35 to 1*. If you're so rich that you can afford such an extreme risk, you have no need of progressive gambling systems. Lucky Number is a fine example of something that works in theory but is utterly unrealistic in practice.

Homework

Play a game of Lucky Number. Enjoy yourself. Pretend you're in a casino and see how much you win. Don't actually try it in a casino, though, unless, once again, it's with someone else's money.

18

Skyline

It may seem to you that I spend all my time working on mathematical gambling systems, but the truth is, it was only a stage in my life that ended with the writing of this book. What I'm really interested in is something extremely different: a universally acceptable definition of sin.

A what? Yes, I know, I get that response from many people, but I'm serious. Think what a bonanza it would be for world peace if only mankind could come up with a universally acceptable definition of sin, one that would be objective and so reasonable and persuasive that everyone everywhere—Christians, Jews, Marxists, atheists, whoever—would be able to refer to it reliably as a standard for their own behavior. Religious people say sin is anything that moves you away from God, but what about atheists and agnostics? How are they supposed to define sin?

I therefore propose a new and universally acceptable definition of sin. From now on, sin is anything that makes your soul smaller. Virtue is anything that makes it larger. With that thought in mind, let's move on to Skyline, our last system.

The System Itself

To play the game of Skyline you'll need a small, portable computer. (The house is gonna love this, I can see it already.) In all frankness, I've never actually played this system, nor would I even try. But theory says Skyline could be played, and it also says it could be the most profitable casino system of all.

Mathematical Analysis

Essentially, a game of Skyline is nothing more than a game of Lucky Number played on all 37 or 38 numbers *simultaneously*. That's where the personal computer comes in: it's not reasonable to expect that any human mind, nor any collection of them that could be fitted around a roulette table, could keep track of 37 or 38 progressions simultaneously. But a small computer could manage it quite nicely. The idea is that by covering every single bet on the table you've got to be winning somewhere. A losing streak in Skyline would amount to a handful of numbers coming up again and again, and another larger handful of numbers not coming up at all.

The real difficulty is on the clerical end: there's only about a minute between spins at most roulette wheels and even if the computer printed out your next bets for you in less than a second it would still be quite a challenge getting 37 or 38 bets counted out and placed on the table—creating a new Skyline—in only 60 seconds.

Accordingly, a serious Skyline player would probably have to have at least a couple of good secretaries.

But you'd better hurry. As of this writing personal computers are still legal (permitted) in the casinos, but there's already so much handwriting on the wall it will likely fall over soon. The class houses will no doubt be the last to ban them but even they could not hold out. It's expecting too much that they would let you use a personal computer on top of everything else.

A Frank Evaluation

Sure. That and UFOs landing on the White House lawn.

Homework

Go back to Lucky Number and note the deepest in the hole we went. Multiply this by 37 or 38. Consider that your charitable contribution to the house.

IV

Blackjack and Baccarat

19

Blackjack and Baccarat

Cards began in ancient times as a divining tool for foreseeing the future. Only later on did it dawn on people that they could be used for game-playing as well. The exact origin is unknown but they're found in one form or another in every part of the world, from the familiar tarot to the Asian tiles to the Native American gaming disks.

Cards reached Europe from the Saracens around the time of the Crusades, possibly brought home by Crusaders but no one knows for sure. What is known is that somewhere along the way they split into two distinct kinds, one for divining, the ancestor of today's tarot, and one for card games, the ancestor of today's familiar 52-card poker deck. Dominos and dice underwent a similar split, the dominos for divining and the dice for gaming, only in the case of dominos the divining aspect fell by the wayside in favor of tarot and the dominos went on to become a whole new kind of game, utterly different from dice, though retaining the same spots.

Nonetheless, the original idea was fortune-telling, not gaming. The Saracen word for cards, *naib*, comes from the Arabic word *nabaa* which, like its Hebrew root *navua*, means "prophecy." Apparently the underlying theory was that God has the power to guide the hand of the person drawing the cards and that He uses this power to cause the reader to draw the cards He desires in order to communicate the message He wants to communicate. This reasoning of course collides head-on with the Biblical prohibition against divining, soothsaying, etc., but evidently the passion to be able to foresee the future was strong enough to cloud minds to this stark, obvious conflict with Biblical injunction.

The same reasoning, interestingly enough, can be applied very persuasively to Chinese fortune cookies. An all-knowing God certainly knows what fortune is contained in each cookie. Likewise He surely has the power to guide a waiter's hand as he's reaching into the fortune cookie box to pull out the correct number of cookies for the party at your table. And of course He can also guide *your* hand as you're reaching for the specific cookie *you* pick. Therefore the question arises: are fortune cookies messages from God?

What a boon it would be for the Chinese restaurant business if this could ever be shown to be the case! In which academic discipline would this be a suitable subject for a dissertation? How would congressional legislators feel about spending taxpayers' money for such research? How strong is the Chinese restaurant lobby?

Today's 52-card deck first appeared in France during the Renaissance. The four kings (from the perspective of late Renaissance France) are representations of the four greatest kings of history, David (spades), Alexander the Great (clubs), Julius Caesar (diamonds), and Charlemagne (hearts). Had it been Great Britain instead of France, the king of hearts would probably be Arthur or Alfred. Had it been the United States or Canada who would he be? You decide. My vote would be for Elvis.

Blackjack is a pleasantly simple game in contrast with baccarat which is so complicated it makes Einstein's Theory of Relativity look pretty straightforward by comparison.

In blackjack the object is to draw cards totaling closer to 21 than the dealer's cards without going over 21. In casino blackjack (as distinct from private blackjack in someone's home) everybody plays against the dealer who is, in effect, "the house," even though it's an actual human being this time, not a roulette wheel or a pair of dice. In other words, it doesn't matter what's happening with the player next to you, it only matters what's happening with the dealer.

In a casino blackjack game the dealer starts the game by dealing everyone at the table two cards, himself included. The Jack, King and Queen each count for 10. The Ace can be either 1 or 11, whichever best suits your hand, and the other cards all count at their face (numerical) value.

If the first two cards dealt you are an Ace and a 10-value card, that's Blackjack and you automatically win unless the dealer also has Blackjack, in which case it's a tie, called a "push" in gambling slang. Actually, anytime you and the dealer have the same totals it's a tie, in which case, naturally, nobody wins.

If you don't have Blackjack on your first two cards, then you can either "stand," which means you do nothing and hope your total is closer to 21 than the dealer's (or hope the dealer draws more cards and goes over 21), or you can ask for a "hit," which means you draw additional cards and hope *you* don't go over 21. Remember, if your cards total over 21, you lose, period, regardless of what's happening with the dealer.

In the years since Vietnam a number of interesting new variations (called "options") have appeared in the game of blackjack and some of the casinos now feature these to make their house more attractive to players than the competition.

Multiple pair splitting, for example, is like traditional pair splitting (where you can split a pair, if you get one, to form two hands) except that it goes a step further and lets you play *three* hands if you split your initial pair and get yet another pair.

Three Sevens is an option that pays 3 to 2 instead of the usual 1 to 1 if you make 21 using any three sevens. If the dealer has Blackjack, though, you still lose. If he has 21 but not Blackjack it's still a tie, no 3-to-2 payoff. Sorry.

Six, Seven, and Eight of the Same Suit Pays 2 to 1 is another new option. The 2-to-1 payoff is indeed very handsome but again you still lose if the dealer has Blackjack and still tie if he has 21, alas. (The casino is a profit-making enterprise, don't forget, not to be confused with the Salvation Army, Sisters of Mercy, etc.)

Late Surrender is an option which allows you to surrender half your wager prior to drawing a third card, provided the dealer doesn't have Blackjack.

Spades is another option where you win 2 to 1. In this case you have to receive a Blackjack consisting of an Ace of Spades and a Jack of Spades. Once again, though, if the dealer gets Blackjack too, *any* Blackjack, it's a tie and your 2-to-1 payoff goes out the window, better luck next time.

Five Card 21 is an interesting mathematical event which also pays 2 to 1. Just as it sounds, you have to make 21 using five cards without the dealer getting Blackjack (in which case you lose) or 21 (in which case you tie).

Of the mathematical gambling systems in this book the one that lends itself most readily to blackjack and baccarat is Half Peak. But you must be cautious because the card games require much larger betting units than craps or roulette, which in turn means much greater risk.

Baccarat is a paradoxical game: the rules are indeed involved. There may not be even fifty people who know them by heart. They may be consulted via a posted notice or a printed card passed out by the house, and yet the game itself might be characterized as the simplest game in the casino.

There are just two contenders in baccarat, the Bankers and the Players. One or the other of them wins, and the payoff is 50–50. What could be easier? (Actually, they could also tie, an 8-to-1 shot. More on this in a moment.)

It would seem, therefore, that the choices of Bankers and Players are like Pass and Don't Pass, and they are, but for one snag: the house betting policy. You see, in craps the house will let you adjust your bet by increments of as little as $1, but in baccarat the minimum increment is $5. You can't bet $7 or $12 or $13 at baccarat the way you can at craps: first of all, the minimum bet is *always* at least $5 or $10, and second of all that minimum $5 increment means your minimum betting *unit* must be at least $5. You may recall I devoted half a chapter earlier on telling you to stick to $1 betting units and not to get greedy and switch to $2 betting units. Yet here all of a sudden we're talking about $5 betting units. This is risk, pal, know it of a certainty.

That much said, a Half Peak game at baccarat would have to begin with an opening bet of, say, $40 (to store a half dozen early wins, in case they come), then increase by $5 after each loss and decrease by $5 after each win. This could be a phenomenally costly game if you ran into a bad losing streak, maybe not as stiff as the navy budget, but close.

This is why (unfortunately) baccarat isn't a practical game for gambling systems. Only very wealthy (or very crazy) people can afford to play a progression at the baccarat table. (James Bond was always playing baccarat but he wasn't playing a progression. He had a much simpler system: he just played the opposite of what the bad guy was playing and since the bad guy always loses, he always won.)

You could consider a limited progression on the 8-to-1 tie, of course. You might, for example, wager $10 + $15 + $20 + $25 = $70 on four hands in a row and if a tie did appear then you'd have a nice profit. Betting four in a row on an 8-to-1 shot gives you a slightly below 50–50 chance of winning, but if you did win, playing with $5 betting units, the profit would be very high, possibly as much as $155. That probably is the most reasonable way of playing a system on the game of baccarat, a limited-risk progression on the 8-to-1 long shot, but even that could have a way of turning out to be a pretty expensive game.

Baccarat is as rigable as any of the other games in the house, don't forget.

Blackjack too, as we mentioned earlier, is a 1-to-1 game, like Pass and Don't Pass. The table minimums are low at blackjack because it's such a popular game. If you come for the action before noon you can often find a $3 table; otherwise expect a minimum of $5. But the house will allow you to shift your bet by as little as $1 from one hand to the next, so you can play with $1 betting units, making Half Peak at a blackjack table the more plausible way to adapt a progressive system to a card game. (If you're using the invisibility method, then you'll play exactly one hand at each table in the place. Use $5, $10 or $25 betting units but set *strict* limits.)

Assuming you're not being invisible and you can find a $3 table, you would open your Half Peak game by betting, say, $9 on the first hand of blackjack. If you win, bet $8 on the second hand. If you lose, bet $10 on the second hand. It's like Half Peak all over again, only you're sitting at a blackjack table instead of standing at a craps table. The only major difference, other than that, is that the pace is slower.

A generation ago a math professor from out West came up with a system for card-counting at blackjack that was so good the houses had to change the rules: back then they dealt cards out of one or two decks; today they deal out of many decks at a time, to make card-counting more difficult, but even now there are memory whizzes counting the cards at blackjack. Some years ago there was an unsightly scandal where a lavish-ly advertised casino dealt an illustrious celebrity a game of blackjack out of only one deck. This amounted to letting him play by more favorable rules than you and I have to play under, which is what the whole ruckus was about. But even without single-deck blackjack there are still card-counters around. If you're good at remembering, card-counting may be for you. The math professor's name was Edward O. Thorpe, and there are no doubt copies of his book still around. He has become a legend, and deservedly so.

Other than card-counting or playing Half Peak at blackjack or baccarat, purely mathematical systems don't lend them-selves well to the card games. As soon as you move into the subjective, such as whether to stand or take a hit at blackjack

or the endless subjective aspects of poker, the purely mathematical systems can't cope. They're like mathematical fish
designed to swim in mathematical streams, and requests for
subjective decisions confuse them and make them unhappy.

But if you can handle the subjective part, then you can play
Half Peak on a blackjack or baccarat table and expect a reasonable chance of success. Try it at home first, as always, and
decide right now that you're going to be invisible.

V

Hedging Craps

20

The Seven Hedge

The dictionary defines *hedge* as, among other things, "an act or means of preventing complete loss of a bet, an argument, an investment, or the like, with a partially counterbalancing or qualifying one." Hedging is an old and familiar concept in the stock market: you buy stock, hoping it will go up, but just in case it fools you and goes down you buy an option giving you the right to sell it for the old price later on, even after it has gone down. The option costs money, of course, but not nearly as much as it saves you if in fact the stock does go down. It's a little like buying insurance: you put out a little extra in premiums, but it's well worth it if things go the wrong way.

This hedging concept has its expression in the science of gambling systems too, only in this case it's the number seven we're concerned about. Seven is the kingpin of the craps table. It's the one number that appears more often than any other, and when it does appear it causes practically every craps system to lose. It follows then that when there happen to be lots of sevens, craps systems do badly. Conversely, when there happen to be unusually few sevens the systems tend to work unusually well.

What we need here, therefore, is a system that thrives when there are lots of sevens: in other words, a system that's a flip-flop of all the other systems, a system that does well when the others are losing, but at the same time doesn't do too badly when all the other systems are winning.

The System Itself

The Seven Hedge is a system designed for the number seven. If you look at fig. 20.1, the Center of the Craps Layout, you'll see a space at the top of the one roll bets (in the center of the layout, just below the Hardway bets) "4 TO 1 ANY SEVEN 4 TO 1." This is exactly what it appears to be, a one-roll proposition bet that the next roll is a seven. If you bet a dollar and the next roll is a seven, you get back your dollar plus four from the house, 4 to 1, in other words. Like Any Craps, the pace is

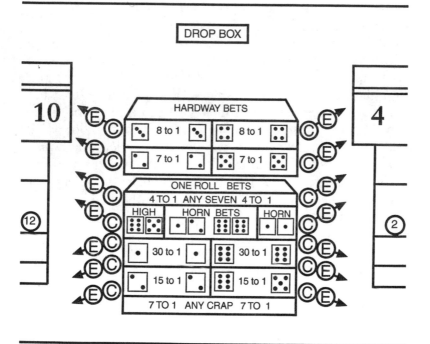

Fig. 20.1. The Center of the Craps Layout

extremely fast, a fresh bet with each new roll of the dice. Note, however, that the true odds are 5 to 1. Remember table 5.1, the dice paradigm: if six out of thirty-six possibilities are a seven, then thirty out of thirty-six possibilities *aren't* a seven. Thus 30 to 6, which equals 5 to 1. This is quite a large slice the house is carving out for itself, a neat 20 percent edge. Contrast it with hard 4/hard 10, a 12.5 percent edge, or hard 6/hard 8, a 10 percent edge, and you can see where the objection arises. By itself Any Seven isn't a very reasonable proposition; however, it offers the singular advantage of paying off at exactly the time when all the other systems lose. So while the Any Seven bet may be no great shakes in and of itself it can nevertheless be extremely helpful as a hedge. Plus, you can dial up exactly the amount of hedging you want just by increasing the size of your betting units.

The Seven Hedge is the same in principle as Any Craps or Baby Hardways. You start with a bet of one dollar (or higher as needed) and add a dollar after every loss until you finally get a seven, then you reduce the bet by $7, $5 because it's a true 5 to 1, plus two extra units to create the critically important drift downward, especially important when you're talking about high betting units (meaning anything over $1). Drift is more important in the case of the Seven Hedge because Any Seven pays only 4 to 1, not 7 to 1 or 9 to 1 like Any Craps or Baby Hardways. This is why the Seven Hedge isn't such an appealing system in its own right; there's no decent multiplication. It's only as a hedge for your other long shots that it comes into its own.

Hedging tends to be confrontational in the sense that there's absolutely no invisibility to it. The house sees exactly what's going on and they will surely notice. This means that if by some mischance you've stumbled into a house that's using a rigged table, hedging will get you thrown out of the place! An honest proprietor wouldn't care, but a dishonest one would have a fit. Your hedging would frustrate his attempt to cheat you!

(Don't go viewing this as a way to beat a dishonest house, if you find one. Better by far just to stay away from such places altogether.)

Mathematical Analysis

So let's take a look at an actual Seven Hedge in operation and see what it looks like.

Table 20.1
The Seven Hedge

Bet No.	Amount	Decision	Total Out	Total In	Profit
1	$1	L	$1		−$1
2	2	L	3		−3
3	3	W	6	$15	9
4	1	L	7		8
5	2	L	9		6
6	3	W	12	30	18
7	1	L	13		17
8	2	W	15	40	25
9	1	W	16	45	29
10	1	L	17		28
11	2	L	19		26
12	3	L	22		23
13	4	L	26		19
14	5	L	31		14
15	6	L	37		8
16	7	L	44		1
17	8	L	52		−7
18	9	L	61		−16
19	10	L	71		−26
20	11	L	82		−37
21	12	L	94		−49
22	13	W	107	110	3
23	6	L	113		−3
24	7	L	120		−10
25	8	L	128		−18
26	9	W	137	155	18
27	2	L	139		16
28	3	L	142		13

BET No.	AMOUNT	DECISION	TOTAL OUT	TOTAL IN	PROFIT
29	4	W	146	175	29
30	1	L	147		28
31	2	L	149		26
32	3	W	152	190	38
33	1	L	153		37
34	2	W	155	200	45
35	1	L	156		44
36	2	L	158		42
37	3	L	161		39
38	4	L	165		35
39	5	L	170		30
40	6	L	176		24
41	7	L	182		17
42	8	W	191	240	49
43	1	L	192		48
44	2	L	194		46
45	3	L	197		43
46	4	L	201		39
47	5	L	206		34
48	6	W	212	270	58
49	1	L	213		57
50	2	L	215		55
51	3	L	218		52
52	4	W	222	290	68
53	1	L	223		67
54	2	L	225		65
55	3	W	228	305	77
56	1	L	229		79
57	$2	W	$231	$315	$85

As you can see, it didn't take long before there was a winner. That's a central feature of the Seven Hedge, you get lots and lots of winners. Unfortunately, they don't pay very much. That too is a central feature of the Seven Hedge. I got four of them in the first nine rolls of the dice, roughly twice as many as probability would predict. By the end of the ninth roll I was already $29 ahead, and this would have been only two or three minutes into the game in an actual casino. But probability caught up with the progression, as you can see, and from bet No. 10 to bet No. 21 there was an eleven-roll drought before another seven appeared, about twice as long as probability says I should have had to wait. Notice that the profit plummeted to –$49 by the twenty-first bet, although the system was back in the black immediately upon winning bet No. 22.

The next win came at bet No. 26. I was –$18 into the hole by bet No. 25, but again, immediately upon winning bet No. 26, I had a profit, this time $18 out of the hole, purely by coincidence. At that point the deficits were gone. For the rest of the game I was in the black, although never excessively so, as you can see. That's one of the hitches of the Seven Hedge. It usually doesn't make much profit unless you use larger-than-average betting units, which you presumably would at a table where unusually many sevens show up, for whatever reason. Again, you needn't conclude that the table is rigged. There could be other reasons why the table gets many sevens, but recognize that all these figures multiply as the betting units multiply.

From bet No. 26 to bet No. 34 there was another streak of luck, winning four out of nine, and the profit, as you can see, jumped all the way to $45. Then it fell off again, all the way back down to $17 before I won again on bet No. 42. From that point on the fundamental profitability of the underlying mathematics began to assert itself, and by the fifty-seventh bet, when I quit, I was $84 ahead, actually an adequate showing for a Seven Hedge.

A Frank Analysis

Well, it's not the pot of gold at the end of the rainbow but it does win when the other systems lose. This is its most notable virtue, more notable, alas, than its profitability. A player who's seeking to be invisible won't bother with the Seven Hedge.

Homework

Play the Hedge alongside Any Craps tonight, both with the same run of dice. Play several games side by side. It should take no more than an hour because they go really fast, both of them.

Now here's the important part. Keep careful track of the number of sevens you get in each game and compare it with the total number of rolls. (A game ends when your Any Craps progression reaches zero again.) What you're looking for is the ratio of the number of sevens to the total number of throws of the dice in each game.

In the games where you have a better-than-average number of sevens, where was the profit—in the Any Craps game or in the Seven Hedge? In the games where you have a smaller-than-average number of sevens, where was the profit—in the Any Craps game or in the Seven Hedge?

21

Hedging Half Peak

First of all, it shouldn't be necessary to hedge a game of Half Peak. In an honest casino Half Peak should turn a very agreeable profit come hell, famine, pestilence, or whatever.

On the flip side, if your overwhelming perception is that the house is dishonest and using wired tables, get out of there. Don't hang out there, and don't allow yourself even to come to their attention.

But in an honest house you can still hit an unlucky streak. So what about hedging Half Peak? Can it be done?

Yes. It's just a simple matter of you or your partner playing a Seven Hedge alongside your Half Peak game. You could also switch from the Pass Line to the Don't Pass line.

There's one more technique for you to consider. Bernard Baruch, in his youth (we touched on this briefly in chapter 4), found a roulette wheel that seemed always to cause the big money to lose. Being a young man of uncommon intelligence, he reasoned that all he would have to do is bet *opposite* the big money and he'd clean up. (What actually happened was that he was soon thrown out of the casino.)

But what about an honest casino? (Or a presumably honest casino.) What happens if on a crowded holiday weekend *nowadays* you simply bet opposite the big money? You see some

high roller throwing down $500 chips on the Pass Line, per-
haps just to impress some Jane he's with. What happens if you
simultaneously throw down $25 chips on Don't Pass?

I don't know. But remember—the size of the bet has no
bearing on the fall of the dice. The little cubes have a mind of
their own.

22

Hedging Hardways

As with Half Peak, it shouldn't be necessary to hedge Baby or Daddy Hardways. As your own home trials will show, the Hardways do just fine entirely on their own, both of them.

But suppose you're at a table which, for reason or reasons unknown, seems to have an unusual number of sevens going by. I wouldn't suggest that your Hardways progression is the reason for all those sevens turning up, but whatever the reason, the fact remains: you've got a problem on your hands. The table is rolling too many sevens. How do you handle it?

Easy. Play a Seven Hedge progression alongside your Hardways progression, but use betting units two or three times larger on the Seven Hedge. If your Hardways progression is using $1 betting units, then try betting $3 units on the Seven Hedge. An honest house will sit still for it. I'm not saying they'll love it, I'm just saying they'll sit still for it.

Hedging is child's play mathematically but very complex on a diplomatic level: The house might feel you're casting aspersions on their character. You wouldn't want to do that any more than you'd want to make snide comments about the French whorehouse decor. You're their guest. Be a gracious guest. Don't make them have to count the silver after you leave.

The best thing to do, certainly the most tactful and diplomatic thing to do, is just to go in there in honest fashion and play your progression, whatever kind it is. And if you discover, once the boxperson sees what you're doing, that there seem to be more sevens than usual, take it as a message from God that it's an unlucky house and move on.

23

Hedging Any Craps

Hedging Any Craps is the same as hedging Baby or Daddy Hardways. You get a fresh bet with each new throw of the dice, remember, the same as your Seven Hedge, so the pace will be vigorous. The Hardways, by contrast, moves so much more slowly that you may get in ten bets or more on your Seven Hedge progression for every *one* bet on your Hardways progression. The Hardways wins also come much more slowly but pay much more.

Once again I point out that it shouldn't be necessary to hedge Any Craps. Try it at home, you'll see exactly what I mean. If you find yourself at a craps table with an improbably high percentage of sevens it may mean the table is wired. Not that you'll ever be able to prove it, of course. Your only "proof" would be that it works at home but not in a casino, and in the eyes of casino management that would still be proof of nothing except that you had an unlucky night. Best not to slander the honest casinos because of any that you might surmise to be otherwise.

24

Hedging Free Odds

Let me remind you that Free Odds was one of those theoretical systems never intended to be played in real life. The problem, you may recall, was that in order to have the necessary flexibility to be able to play the free odds progressions adequately you had to have a staggeringly high bankroll riding on either Pass or Don't Pass, and this in turn would necessarily leave you fearfully vulnerable to a killer losing streak.

But suppose you just won the lottery and couldn't care less about killer losing streaks, what then? How, mathematically, does one hedge the Free Odds, all the risks and perils being fully understood up front?

You would hedge it, theoretically at least, by just an ordinary Seven Hedge progression, but with phenomenally high betting units, probably $10 or more. Your Seven Hedge progression would have to be $10, $20, $30, $40, etc., followed by a $70 reduction in the amount of your Seven Hedge bet after every win.

Is this practical? It is, but only until you hit a bad losing streak.

Just as Free Odds itself must be judged impractical, likewise an attempt to hedge the free odds must be judged impractical.

But by the same token, just as the Free Odds can be a marvelous study and provide a whole new insight into the mathematical underpinnings of the various craps systems, likewise an attempt to hedge the free odds (at home on your kitchen table, please) can broaden that study and deepen the insight into craps systems.

VI

Hedging Roulette

25

The Red-and-Black Hedge

To explain the Red-and-Black Hedge we'll have to return to the overall roulette layout for a moment, fig. 10.1. It's the same layout for both single and double-zero roulette, only the zeros change from one to the other. By now this diagram should be familiar to you, but there's a hidden subtlety lurking here in the arrangements of the red and black numbers all through the inside, as shown in fig. 10.1.

If you count them you'll find there are precisely eighteen red numbers and eighteen black numbers. This is as you would expect, since red and black are both 1-to-1 bets. But if you look closely you'll see there's a gross unevenness in the *distribution* of the reds and blacks throughout the columns. The first column is the only one that has an equal number of reds and blacks, six each. The second column is totally lopsided, with eight blacks but only four reds. And the third column is just as lopsided, with eight reds but only four blacks.

It follows from this that any run of numbers that contains an above-average number of blacks will tend very strongly to be a better-than-average run for the second column because while the second column contains only twelve out of the thirty-six possible numbers, or 33 percent, it contains eight out of the eighteen possible black numbers, or 44 percent.

153

Thus, if you're sitting there playing a game of Two-Step on the middle column at a time when there are a good number of blacks coming by, your Two-Step game is probably going to do pleasantly well.

But what if you're sitting there playing Two-Step on the middle column and lots of reds come by? Your Two-Step game in this case is probably going to do more losing than winning and your losses will tend to be disagreeably high.

Now if ever there was a situation that cried out for hedging, this is it. Instead of just sitting there alone playing Two-Step on the middle column, you recruit a buddy to sit there with you and keep you company, only he plays a 1 to 1 Half Peak game on the red while you're playing a 2-to-1 Two-Step game on the middle column. This way, if there's an average mix of blacks and reds, you both make money. If there's an above-average number of reds, he makes an above-average amount of money on his 1-to-1 Half Peak game on the reds, to offset the losses you're probably suffering in your 2-to-1 Two-Step game on the middle column. And if there's a disproportionate number of blacks instead, then your Two-Step game makes an above-average amount of money to offset the losses he's suffering in his 1-to-1 Half Peak game on the reds.

This is the mathematical buffering effect known as the Red-and-Black Hedge, and it works just as well pairing a Two-Step game on the third column with a Half Peak game on the black, for the same reason. Any run that has a disproportionate number of reds will favor the Two-Step game on the third column because while it has only 12 of the 36 possible numbers, or 33 percent, it has 8 of the 18 possible red numbers, or 44 percent. And any run that doesn't have a reasonable number of reds, while it may make your Two-Step game on the third column difficult, must necessarily be profitable for your buddy's Half Peak game on the black.

The Red-and-Black Hedge is just chapter 4 played alongside chapter 10 at the same roulette wheel. The two systems complement each other nicely when played this way. The important thing to remember is which pairs fit. Just match the color that appears *least* often in the column with that same color over on the 1 to 1. Think of it as balancing them out. Thus, the middle column, which is short of reds, gets paired with the red, while the third column, which is short of blacks, gets paired with the black. That way somebody's got to be covered, no matter which color predominates in the actual numbers that turn up on the wheel.

The best preparation for a pair of partners for the Red-and-Black Hedge is to have one of them become thoroughly familiar with Half Peak and the other to become thoroughly familiar with Two-Step, then go pick out their wheel. But if it's only one player and a hedge can't be arranged for lack of a partner, then the system of choice must be Holistic Roulette, the best roulette system anyway, and an interesting mathematical cousin of the Any Craps system we learned at the craps table back in chapter 7.

26

Hedging All Others

The essence of this chapter is the two-number bet on 0 and 00. What happens if you build a simple, $1 betting unit progression on the 0/00 bet?

Mathematically it amounts to a game of Holistic Roulette IV, but on the two-number bet only, not the three-number "street" bet. Your odds, as always, are 17 to 1, a very good deal considering the true odds are 18 to 1. But beware—if you hit even a modest losing streak at 17 to 1, it's a disaster. One thing you won't have to worry about, though, is a rigged table because in roulette the rig always *favors* the zeros. As always you should assume the house is honest, but if it's not, your two-number progression on 0/00 is going to get you thrown out. Should you then tell the media? It depends on your sense of humor.

Since the odds are so long you simply *must* limit yourself to $1 betting units.

Other than that it's exactly as you would expect. Play any or all of the roulette systems as you please. When zeros turn up your roulette systems will lose, but your two-number progression on 0/00 will make money hand over fist—17 to 1. Wait'll the first time you hit on a 17 to 1. You and God will meet and talk face to face, as friend with friend.

The 0/00 is a fine approach to hedging Two-Step, Trilogy, or any of the Holistic Roulette systems, and you could even play a whole new kind of Harvesting the Zeros by betting a two-number progression on 0/00 instead of separate bets on 0 and 00, although Harvesting the Zeros, I remind you, is another of those theoretical systems, good for analysis only, not for real life.

Bring a partner. It will spare you the mental strain of trying to manage two separate, complicated progressions at once. If you're trying to stay invisible, then choose a partner of a different age, sex, ethnicity and style of dress from you. You could even make a totally separate game of seeing how long it takes the house to catch on, with a separate sub-game of seeing what happens when they do.

VII

Capital

27

Capital and Low-Capital Variations

Ah, capital, what magic stuff it is. Karl Marx was so fascinated with it that he actually founded a religion based on it. Capital is what makes the world go round, never mind all that other nonsense about love, inertia, or whatever. It's capital that really does it, and if you think otherwise it's only because you've never had your hands on any of it.

Capital is the heart and soul of all gambling systems. So far in this book we've looked at lots of interesting formulas and combinations of formulas, but they're only the foam on top of the wave. The wave itself is capital, and the name of the game is to keep it growing. Capital is your only safety. It's your very survival. As long as you have capital, you can handle anything. The moment you run out of it you're dead, ice-cold dead on the slab, and there's nothing that can bring you back except more capital.

Instead of figuring out how to get more capital it's much easier not to run out of it in the first place. Happily, that's not hard to do. You just have to be sure you have enough to start with, and to play with the smaller betting units until you get sufficient reserves built up. That last part is the hard part: you, being human, are likely to get greedy and spend long hours contemplating the fact that you can double your profit just by increasing your betting units from $1 to $2. That, of course, is what's going to get you into trouble, but there's no need for me to belabor this point. The wise will listen, the foolish will go down in a blaze of glory. Many go each way.

The system player's biggest problem is capital. A game of Half Peak or any other casino system can go on forever and the player can never lose as long as he has the capital to hang in there. But the moment he runs out of capital he's dead. He can no longer maintain the progression that would eventually have brought him back all his capital and more, when his luck finally did change. Your only safety lies in keeping your capital growing, endlessly and forever, eternally heightening and strengthening the dikes against the storm of bad luck that could one day come. Could and probably sooner or later must.

How much capital does it take? Who knows? Your problem is the ever-recurring losing streak. Not only can it happen to you, but if you continue playing for any great length of time it becomes inevitable. The only way a system player can deal with it is to have enough reserve capital to see it through.

But what about the guy who's got just a hundred dollar bill? What kind of chance has he got in this high-capital business of system gambling? Happily again, the majority of these systems have low-capital versions that can be played at the outset with as little as a $10 bill and it's much less wear and tear on your nerves.

The essence of all these low-capital variations is loss limitation: you begin with only a certain amount of money, however much you choose, and that's it. There's no more to lose because you're simply not going to put up any more than that, and if it works, fine, and if it doesn't, that's fine too. Your loss is limited in advance, usually to a minuscule amount of money compared to what we've been talking so far. There's actually an extreme variation that requires as little as $6, but first let's go back and review quickly some of the more adaptable systems in this book in the order we learned them, only this time with an eye toward possible low-capital variations.

Half Peak has its own low-capital variation based on something called the "ding factor." It's named after the bell that dings on a pinball machine when you win extra points. The ding in the case of Half Peak is the extra money you win, the sudden surge in your profit-per-bet every time your progression bottoms out against the house minimum. The idea is no longer to design a progression which will average one-half unit of profit-per-bet over the long run. Rather, the idea becomes to design a progression which will bottom out against the house minimum at least once or twice in a very short run of bets, usually no more than six or seven.

You will recall how Half Peak works: it's a simple Alembert progression, increasing by $1 after every loss, decreasing by $1 after every win. In a normal game you would make your opening bet at least $6 to $7 above the house minimum in order to be able to store up your early good luck, if you have any. But in the low-capital version you don't worry about storing anything because the whole game's only going to last for six or seven bets or so. You start right at the minimum and hope you win immediately. If you do, and it's a $3 table, say, then instead of winning your customary one-half unit per bet you win $3. You can't correct down to $2 after winning because the house won't let you, it's a $3 table, so instead, if it should be a winning streak, you just sit there and keep winning $3, bet after bet, more than they'd be losing to you if they let you reduce your bet down to $2, then $1.

If you lose you increase to $4, and if you lose again you increase to $5, but that's it: $3 + $4 + $5 = $12 is your limit. If your luck is in the wrong direction then you lose no more than $12 and quit. If you want to try again you start all over at the minimum.

This works much better on a $5 or $10 table, although the required stake is that much higher, $18 or $33, instead of $12.

You walk up to a $10 table, say, with the idea in mind that only one of two things is going to happen: either (1) you're going to bet six or seven bets and quit or (2) you'll lose your $33 before you reach the sixth or seventh bet. If luck is with you and you get more winners than losers, you have won back all your losses, plus one-half unit per bet, plus at least one and maybe two or more dings of $10 each for each time your progression hits bottom against the $10 minimum and can't be corrected lower.

Extreme good luck yields $60 or $70 profit while extreme bad luck loses only $33, yet the likelihood of one versus the other is 50–50. What will happen the majority of the time is that you'll reach the sixth or seventh bet and quit before running through the $33 stake. If you had more wins than losses then you ding at least once and make a nice profit. If not, you have a net loss. But in no case can you lose more than $33, if you're playing a $10 table, or $18 at a $5 table, or $12 at a $3 table. Loss limitation is the key.

Any Craps offers a different situation. Here we're playing a 7-to-1 long shot, and yet the concept is the same: loss limitation. If all you have is a $10 bill then all you can bet is $1 + $2 + $3 + $4 = $10, or four bets in a row. With a 7-to-1 shot, four bets in a row ought to be enough to pull in a winner about half the time. If not, you quit at $4 and limit the total loss to $10. You don't make that fifth bet of $5. It would increase your expenses by 50 percent to make that fifth bet, $15 instead of $10, but your chances of winning it are only 7 to 1. Therefore it's wise to just not make it. Better to limit your losses to a maximum of $10.

This reasoning is sometimes taken yet a step further. If you limit your progression to only three bets then your total risk is only $1 + $2 + $3 = $6. Your chances of winning are one-fourth less but your maximum possible loss is four-tenths less, 25 percent versus 40 percent. The worst that can happen is that you lose $6, but if you win a 7 to 1 on $1, say, you have $7 profit; if you win on $2 you have $13 profit; and if you win on $3 you have $18 profit. With a relatively short long shot like the 7-to-1 on Any Craps your chances of winning in three tries are still fairly reasonable, four to nine, or four times out of every thirteen attempts. But again, if you lose, all you lose is $6.

In spite of the theoretical edge of $1 + $2 + $3 over $1 + $2 + $3 + $4, I would prefer to try four in a row rather than just three in a row. The risk jumps to $10, but the payoff comes more often and is much more profitable if the winner comes on the $4 bet, which it does every fourth win, statistically, or every thirty-second bet placed.

As it is with Any Craps, so it is with Baby Hardways, Daddy Hardways, and the Seven Hedge. In every case the idea is to start a normal progression at $1 but follow through for only three, four or five bets, as you choose.

At roulette all this thinking goes out the window because the roulette dealer won't let you bet just $1. He's got a $3 minimum, unlike the craps dealer, so at roulette you have to try three progressions at once, risking $10 (or $6) on each. Either that or switch to a $3 betting unit, which is three times as expensive.

Roulette for this reason is an unfavorable game for very low-capital systems. Your best hope would be simply to search out a $3 wheel and then play three six-number bets at once. If the bets all lose, which should happen about 50 percent of the time, play only two six-number bets of $2 each. If both of these lose, then play $3 on only one six-number bet. If that loses, quit. Limit your total losses to $10 again while affording a reasonable chance to win at least that much and maybe more.

Any Craps, Baby and Daddy Hardways, and all the rest of the long-shot craps systems can all be played as a simple $1 + $2 = $3, and theoretically there may be no more efficient way to do it. Thus, if you're looking for the best low-capital gambling system it may be just that, to keep betting $1, then $2 on the long shot of your choice. Your total risk is never more than $3 but your potential profit (on a 7 to 1) is as much as

$13. Half of all the times you win you'll win $13. The other half you'll win $7, which means your average win is $10, when you win. How often do you win? On a 7 to 1 (a true 8 to 1) you'll win a little less than a quarter of the time. You'll pay an average of a little over $12 to win an average of $10—a net loss, in other words.

Thus, when you check out the figures carefully you discover that *none* of the low-capital variations gives you as good a deal mathematically as the high-capital version of the same game. That's true. If it were otherwise, there'd be no point in bothering with the high-capital versions.

So we discover in the end that we're best off avoiding the low-capital systems if possible, but if not then take your pick: bet just two in a row and risk only $3, then quit; or if you like, three in a row and risk only $6, then quit; or four and risk $10; or five and risk $15; or even six and risk $21. But somewhere in there and somewhere early on, remember to quit—the earlier the better. Otherwise you won't be limiting your losses, and limiting loss in the essence of every low-capital variation. Unless you remember to limit your losses, it won't be low-capital.

VIII

Still More Systems

28

Traditional Systems

The science of gambling systems probably goes back to ancient times, and the traditional systems include some fine and impressive attempts to use human genius to foil the odds.

We've already looked at Alembert, which is the foundation of Half Peak. By itself Alembert is a pretty nice way to study the tides of probability, the ebb and flow of luck. You can just stand there and ride the waves up and down forever, collecting half a unit per bet profit the whole time, calmly monitoring your own drift upward until it finally outdistances your capital, which it inevitably must, and wipes you out. Alembert, because of drift, must necessarily be a short-term system: you play it in a casino for just an hour or two, or just a single evening, and if luck is with you you win slightly more than you would have if you'd merely been betting random chance. If luck isn't with you you still lose, of course, but the Alembert progression, by virtue of its steady half-unit per bet profit, softens the blow and causes you to lose less than you would have. Either that or it lets you play an unlucky streak a little further than you otherwise might have.

One of the best known of the traditional systems is Martingale, also known as Double-Up. It's played on an even money bet, say, Pass or Don't Pass at craps, or any of the 1-to-1 bets at roulette, or at blackjack.

169

You begin by betting $1. If you lose you bet $2, then $4, then $8, etc., doubling after each loss until you finally win, at which time you have $1 profit. The math of this is very convincing if you don't look too deeply: $1 + $2 + $4 + $8 = $15, but when the $8 bet wins you pick up $16 off the table, giving you your $1 profit. You've lost three bets and won one, yet you're a dollar ahead. Plus, it holds for any length of progression. No matter how many times you lose and double your bet, you still win it all back again plus $1 when you finally do win. The flaw is that the geometric progression expands so fast that when you eventually hit a hairy losing streak you very quickly run out of capital or run up against the house limit, one or the other, and suffer tremendous loss. That's what's shallow about the mathematical argument in favor of Martingale. Probability says that every six months or so you're going to hit a run of *fourteen* straight losses. If you work that out on your calculator you'll see it amounts to a bet of $16,384. This is already higher than the house limit in most casinos, and if you should happen to hit a losing streak of *fifteen* in a row, which probability says ought to occur at least once a year, then we're talking about a bet of $32,768. All that, just to win $1.

Nonetheless, there are said to be successful Martingale players around, and if there are I can tell you sight unseen their secret is loss limitation. They don't keep doubling and doubling and doubling to infinity, they quit after a while, probably after just four or five bets. Sometimes after just three. If they lose that many in a row they just quit and swallow the loss rather than risk twice as much trying to win back that basic one dollar. People who play Martingale this way probably have some chance of survival but for a serious system player all this swallowing is no way to go about the business of accumulating capital.

The other great traditional casino system is Labouchere, also known as Cancellation, a favorite old warhorse. It seems to get taken out and dusted off every twenty years or so and paraded around as a new invention, usually in an article in a magazine with a young editor, but it's actually been around for centuries, too. Labouchere seems to work magic by making each win gobble up two losses, but when you look behind the smoke and mirrors you realize the whole thing's done with very high betting units, and as soon as you hit your first spell of bad luck Labouchere will bankrupt you just as any system will if played with unreasonably high betting units.

Here's how it works. You make a short vertical list of numbers, say

1

2

3

and bet the sum of the top and bottom numbers, in this case $1 + $3 = $4. If you lose you enter the amount you lost at the bottom of the list, then once again bet the sum of the top and bottom numbers, now $1 + $4 = $5. If you win, you cross off the top and bottom numbers then bet the sum of the top and bottom of the remaining numbers.

You do this only on even-money bets—Pass, Don't Pass, etc.

It appears that your list adds a number each time you lose, but loses two numbers every time you win, therefore with an even-money, 1-to-1 bet your whole list must inevitably get crossed out eventually, leaving you with a profit equal to the sum of the original list, in this case, $6.

This is true, but as soon as you hit three winners the top number in your list is no longer a light and simple $1, $2, or $3. Instead it's some much larger number, plus you're adding it to an even larger number somewhere down at the bottom to get the amount of your actual bet. Given a few splashes of bad luck in a system like this, you can quickly run into the same problem as any other player who's chosen unwisely large betting units; you either run out of capital or find yourself having to make stupendous and ever-larger wagers to keep the system going. Labouchere can be a charming system on a night where you're running into average luck, but on a bad night it will leave you totally wrecked.

The most absurd of the traditional systems is Maturity of the Chances. This system is an imbecile's feast, so obviously ludicrous that it's hard to see why anyone would rely on it at all. Yet *it's the most popular roulette system there is,* even more popular than Martingale, and there are a lot of craps shooters who swear by it, too. The Maturity of the Chances systems is based on the fallacy that, since things tend to even up in the long run, you can predict the next bet by keeping track of what's just appeared. In other words, if you're sitting there at a roulette table and the ball has landed on red numbers the past three times in a row, then it means a black number is due. Or if there have been three straight passes at craps, it means a Don't Pass is due.

No, it doesn't mean that at all, but to the believer in the Maturity of the Chances system the mathematical reality means nothing. To him it seems to make sense, in much the same way as the idea that the earth is flat seems to make sense.

In fact, the odds are what they are. They don't change because the three previous turns have been reds, or the three previous shooters have passed. The roulette wheel has no memory, nor have the dice. The person who plays Maturity of the Chances is in truth merely betting random chance. If he's lucky he'll win, and if he isn't he'll lose, that's all.

Keeping records of what has or hasn't shown at roulette or craps is a waste of time. Yet you can go to any casino on a weekend and see people carefully recording all the numbers at a roulette wheel until they spot one that hasn't shown in a hundred turns or so. They then start betting that one, turn after turn, on the grounds that "it's due." The hell it's due! That's as damned fool a notion as you'll ever run across. I've never yet seen a roulette wheel with a schedule posted on its side like a train station. There's no such thing as "due." Yet the common sense aspect of this system, like the common sense aspect of a flat earth, the fact that it really does seem as though it ought to be so, makes this system a perennial favorite. And if such players lose they'll say it was bad luck, and if they win they'll say, "Of course! It was due!"

The traditional systems are for fun only, not for serious system playing. This might be an appropriate occasion to remind you that the heart and soul of every successful gambling system is capital and keeping it growing, and that, unfortunately, is the one thing none of the traditional systems is particularly reliable at.

29

A Good Horse System

Horse players will want to know if any of these systems can be applied to the racetrack. The answer is no because the situation at the racetrack lacks the uniformity of the situation in the casino. The dice or the roulette wheel present exactly the same mathematical situation every time. The horses at the track, by contrast, have no uniformity whatsoever. Not only do you get a different mix of horses in every race but the individual horses themselves vary from race to race, some days having a good day, some days having a bad day, much the same as human beings.

Does this mean it's impossible to approach the racetrack mathematically the way we've approached the casinos mathematically? No, it just means progressive betting is impossible.

So what other kind of betting is there? Well, in this case there's a whole new approach and it's called shopping the pools for bargains.

Shopping the what for what? This will take some explaining.

Let's begin with your daily newspaper. Does it have a horse page? If it doesn't you can always pick up a copy of the *Daily Racing Form*. I happen to live in New York City where the *Daily News* has one of the finest horse pages in the country. Every day six experts pick the day's winners in advance. Do they get it right every time? Of course not. In fact, not only do they *not* get it right every time, on most days they don't even agree with one another. One expert'll pick Federal Sam to win in the fourth, and the expert right next to him will say no way, Federal Sam's gonna place behind Aunt Ruthie's Mink. And yet another expert meanwhile will say they're both wrong, Moysh the Nose is gonna take it by ten lengths, etc., etc.

So who's right? That's the secret! *They all are!* No, the experts don't pick a winner every time, but all of them pick an unquestionably better-than-average horse *always,* and that's how you win at the racetrack. You just pull the horse page from your morning paper and in each race make a list of the names of every horse that the experts said had a chance of finishing in the money, not merely Win, but Place and Show as well. All such horses you designate as "contenders," then it's just a simple matter of hanging by the betting window in the last minute or two before the race as the betting pools close and watching the television screen to see what the closing odds are on each of the contenders.

Most of the time your contenders will have very short odds, 1 to 1, 5 to 4, 3 to 2, etc., because they're favorites, but every now and then, for no comprehensible reason, a contender will be available at amazingly long odds, sometimes 10, 15, or even 20 to 1. You'll stand there watching the screen and your jaw will drop. A man who knows enough about horses to get his picks published in the *New York Daily News* says the horse is one of the good ones, and yet there it is on the screen being offered at *20 to 1!*

Now do you see? *The final odds on a horse as the betting pools close have nothing whatever to do with the quality of the horse. They're merely a reflection of how the fickle public happens to be betting in that particular race.*

So that's when you place your bet. If it's just an ordinary long shot, bet the pony to Show. If it's a very long shot, bet *two* bets, one to Show and one to Place. And if it's a very, very long shot, bet *three* bets, one to Show, one to Place and one to Win. Every now and then you'll win all three. In such moments you will know the Lord.

Most of the time you'll lose, just as with the casino long shots, but the times when you win, your long shot will pay $20, $25, maybe even $30 on a two-dollar bet, more than enough to make up for all the times your long-odds contenders didn't win.

Once you get the hang of it with $2 bets try doing it with $100 bets. If you're successful and start to win serious money, see it as a sign from God that He wants you to switch to $500 or $1,000 bets. But never bet more than a grand no matter how long the odds because you'll start to become conspicuous and people will begin to notice you, and this in the end will probably be unhelpful. Do you remember that magic word *invisible?* In life it's generally a wise idea to keep your private business private.

And that's it. That's your horse system. As you can see, it's purely mathematical in spite of its being non-progressive. There's no subjective dimension whatsoever. The horses could be made of metal for all the difference it would make. You're not betting on horses, you're betting on the public to have made a mistake when it shied away from a better-than-average horse for no good reason. If you want to, you can even go down to the paddock between races and look at the horses up close. Thoroughbred ponies are among the most gorgeous of God's creations.

30

The Ultimate System: The Cockroach System

The ultimate system is to get God on your side. But how? This must be one of the most carefully studied questions of all time. How indeed? Any system which could do this would surely be the ultimate system, I'm sure you'll agree.

So how do you do it? How do you get God on your side? The Bible offers a strong clue: "You shall love the Lord your God with all your heart and all your soul and all your might." Is this a command, or a prediction of a future state of affairs, or both?

Is love what He wants, then? Is that what it takes to get God on your side, for you to love Him? If so, it immediately raises the question, how can you make yourself feel love? We can't force ourselves to feel love any more than we can force ourselves to feel trust. It's one of those things where you either feel it or you don't. If loving God is what it takes to get Him on your side, then how do you make yourself feel love?

The problem is that love, like trust, comes from the *unconscious*, which is by definition inaccessible to the conscious will or volition.

So then how do you do it? How do you make your unconscious love God, or at least begin to love God, at least to start
moving in that direction?

This raises the old question of how do you bring the bull in
from the pasture?

The answer is, you *don't* bring the bull in from the pasture.
You bring the *cows* in from the pasture and the bull follows
the cows.

It's much the same with the human unconscious mind. You
can safely rely on it to follow the cows, in this case the conscious mind. If the conscious mind forms the habit of regularly recognizing the reality of God, the unconscious will see and
understand and will itself eventually come around to recognizing the reality of God. At that point you experience what the
psalmist called "the joyful shout," and feel as if you've been
born again, but all of what's really happened is that your
*un*conscious mind has awakened to the reality of God and His
presence in the space in and around you. This in turn is a
major step on the road to getting God on your side. So use
your free will to steer your conscious mind in the right direction and your unconscious mind will sooner or later follow just
as surely as the bull sooner or later follows the cows in from
the pasture.

Now all this may be an oversimplification, unfortunately,
because there's at least some inferential evidence that free will,
like perhaps the tables in some few of the casinos, may actually be rigged, only in this case by none other than God Himself.

Suppose I invite you to dinner. I want to offer you a choice
of beef, lamb, or chicken and I want you to have free will in
deciding. But let's say I happen to be overloaded with chicken
at the moment, while also happening to be a little short of
both the beef and the lamb. So I'd actually rather you ate the
chicken and stayed away from the beef and lamb. But at the
same time I want you to have completely free will. How can I
do it?

Consider the sauces, and the choice of which kind. Let's say I happen to know you love honey sauce. Let's say I also happen to know you don't care for onion sauce at all, nor for garlic sauce. So what happens if you come for dinner and I say, "Hey, I've got three choices for you, beef with onion sauce," to which you turn up your nose, "or lamb with garlic sauce," to which you turn up your nose again, "or chicken with honey sauce," and immediately your face lights up at the words "honey sauce" and you say, "Oh yeah, I'll have the chicken with the honey sauce, please!"

Did you have free will? Yes, you did. Nothing stopped you from selecting the beef or the lamb. You could have. And yet you didn't, and the reason was the sauce. It was rigged. I knew what the outcome would be when I recited the list of sauces. And yet at no time did I take away your free will. You had completely free will the whole time.

That's how God does it with us. He gives us free choice, but every choice is based on two lists, one why you should and one why you shouldn't, and He decides the contents of each list. He makes sure the one He wants you to pick is the more persuasive one and He sweetens it however much it takes to make sure. Once you realize this, you don't have free will anymore. It disappears and is replaced by a contemplation of the lists and a clear realization that you're being steered. Free will is genuine, but only until you learn to spot the sauce. From then on you realize everything's rigged.

Of course it's rigged. It's *His* universe. Whose universe did you think it was?

Not everyone can grasp this for some reason. There are evidently two kinds of people in this world, one kind who can grasp it and one kind who can't. Like the idea that a Communist could pretend to be a Democrat or Republican and deliberately spend the government into bankruptcy, pretending all the while it was to help people and make the world a better place. There are some people who can grasp it immediately and some who just cannot grasp it no matter if you talk to them all day. It has nothing to do with intelligence or brains or IQ. It's *largeness*. It's a matter of the largeness of the vessel that is your soul. Once you finally get it large enough you float like a balloon up to a higher quantum level of perception, what Kabbalists call a higher world, from which all kinds of new things suddenly become apparent. Like the realization that an invisible God actually is watching you every second of your life. He's watching you now as you're reading the words on this page, just as He was watching me as I wrote them, wondering if I was going to give Him a line in the credits somewhere, at least a word or two squeezed in between the Cameraman and the Key Grip maybe. You realize He's an active participant in your life even when you're not mindful of His being there. Especially when you're not mindful of His being there. You also realize He must have plans, and that while many of them are outside human comprehension, not all of them are, by any means. You realize a lot of amazing things.

So getting back to Square One again, how do you get God on your side?

It depends which quantum level you're on, which world. If you're on the standard quantum level and think free will is real, then the way to get God on your side is by making the right choices and passing your moral tests. These are important. Don't pooh-pooh them or you'll blow it. Passing them will make you steadily larger. A day will come when you will know a joyful shout.

If your perspective is on the higher quantum level, the higher world, then you realize everything's rigged, and since it is, our original question of how do you make your unconscious mind love God becomes irrelevant, because you now realize it's rigged by *Him* whether or not you're going to love Him. Instead the question becomes, how do you become one of His favorites so He'll rig the lists for *you*?

By taking an interest in Him, apparently. Maybe you can't force yourself to love Him but you can certainly take an interest in Him and this evidently is what He responds to, the same as you or I. (That much done it might also be helpful to ask Him to make it plain what He wants and do your best to do it, or to explain as articulately as you can what the cause for your unwillingness is. He evidently responds very generously to this.)

God's goal is to get everybody's soul to the higher quantum level so that the recognition of His reality, the knowledge of Him, will fill the earth as the waters cover the sea, as Isaiah put it. Eventually this will actually happen, it's not just the ramblings of some wackos from the Bible Belt. When the last of the spiritual pollution is gone there'll be nothing making souls smaller anymore. Instead they'll all be getting steadily larger, every last one on earth. A day will come when they'll float up out of their present world like balloons and ascend to a new place altogether.

We live our whole lives as vulnerable to being squished as cockroaches on a kitchen counter. Do we realize it any more than the cockroaches do? They're actually fascinating creatures, these unfairly maligned cockroaches, and they're far more gracious and charming than their critics would have you believe. The cockroaches may have the worst public relations of any creature in the animal kingdom. Even the snakes get better press than the cockroaches. The night that I was doing the first draft of this chapter I was heating spaghetti sauce for dinner, the supermarket had a new kind on sale, and I decided to try it, and because of the subject matter of what I was writing about (cockroaches on my kitchen counter), I decided not to wipe up a small spill of the sauce but rather to leave it for the cockroaches to enjoy. I normally set out all kinds of poison disks for them, their grace and charm notwithstanding, but there's always one or two of them still around regardless, so in a burst of heightened consciousness I decided to leave some of the spaghetti sauce for them.

I had dinner, forgot about the cockroaches completely, but noticed that the sauce, while delicious, was making me unusually thirsty. I found myself drinking glass after glass of water.

Later that night I returned to the kitchen, saw a cockroach on the counter and suddenly remembered. Was he eating the spilled sauce, I wondered? Slowly, carefully, I stepped over to see. No. He wasn't near the sauce. Had he tasted it? I couldn't say for sure. Until I looked again and realized what he was doing. He was parked right by the edge of a large drop of spilled water, drinking and drinking, thirsty without end.

The cockroaches don't see us, do they? They don't know we're there. But suppose one day a cockroach came along who *did* see you, who looked up from the kitchen counter and actually realized you were there, and was curious about you. You sure wouldn't squish that one, would you? No, indeed. Why, he'd be the most interesting cockroach you ever saw in all your life. You'd open the refrigerator door, quickly size up the very best of the delicacies present and sprinkle tiny bits and pieces all around the kitchen counter and hope that he would at least go for some of them.

But the cockroach doesn't see us, alas. He has eyes, and they most certainly do see. Does he have ears? Does he hear us talking? I know he doesn't understand human language but does he at least hear sounds in the air? What does he think they are?

So he does have eyes, and they do see, and yet they don't see *us*. What's the problem?

The problem isn't with the eyes, it's with the soul inside. It isn't large enough to comprehend. He has the sense organ needed but that isn't enough. How much the same with us. We also have the sense organ needed but in our case it isn't the eyes, it's the heart. The organ pulls in the data, but we have no idea what we're perceiving. The soul isn't large enough to comprehend.

So you see, we really are very much like that cockroach. It's just a matter of quantum levels, higher and lower worlds. Fully four hundred of them, according to the Holy Kabbalah. Quite a balloon ride. We live our whole lives on God's kitchen counter except for when we finally wake up and realize He's there watching us. Once we do that we don't live on His kitchen counter anymore, we live in the palm of His hand.

The Cockroach System is just a matter of being one of those special cockroaches. Then suddenly you find yourself winning lotteries you didn't even buy tickets for. It's the one system that always beats the house and it's even easier than progressive gambling systems. Except of course for that voice in your mind, the doubtful one that says, "Eh, very charming, but it wouldn't really work."

If you're stuck in that world and just plain can't get out of it, then I say get back to your kitchen table and really get it together with the math. You can still be in on it but you have to get the math together. Totally. And also, remember to be invisible.